Beckenham

*An Anthology of Local History
to celebrate the Golden Jubilee
of Beckenham's Charter of
Incorporation, 1935.*

Edited by
JOHN WAGSTAFF AND DORIS PULLEN

*with an introduction by Sir Philip Goodhart, MP for Beckenham
1957-1992.*

Reprinted with additions 1994 by

ABLE PUBLISHING SERVICES
9, Station Road, Knebworth,
Hertfordshire. SG3 6AP

Acknowledgements

The Editors express sincere thanks to the many contributors to this book – all of them local residents past or present – who have so willingly given their services. We are particularly indebted to the Historical Association and to members of the Beckenham Branch for their generous assistance in launching this project, upon which much helpful advice was given by staff of the Bromley Central Library. Beckenham Historical Association member Mrs Joyce Moore very kindly typed the manuscripts.

The sources of the photographs are indicated adjacent to their accompanying captions, but a special word of thanks is due to Mrs Kathleen Walters (nee Garnham), who provided some of the pre-war views of the High Street. The line drawings, including the cover picture, are by George V.R. Pullen.

JSW DEP 1984

The publication of a pamphlet by the Historical Association does not necessarily imply the Association's official approval of the opinions expressed in it.

ISBN 0 85278 275 6

HA 3/2/85

Originated and published by the Historical Association, 59a Kennington Park Road, London, SE11 4JH, and printed in Great Britain by Chameleon Press Ltd., 5-25 Burr Road, London, SW18 4SG.

Contents

About The Beckenham Historical Association

Most of those who have been involved in the preparation of this book are members of the Beckenham and Bromley Branch of the Historical Association. Meetings are held generally on one Thursday of each month in the Beckenham Day Centre, when lectures are given by distinguished speakers on topics of local, national and international interest. A monthly news-letter is circulated, a variety of visits are arranged, and the Branch holds an Annual Dinner in February.

Membership details and copies of the Programme, which runs from September to June, may be obtained from the Hon. Membership Secretary (please consult the staff of Beckenham Reference Library or of the Local Studies Section of Bromley Central Library for particulars).

1994 addendum.

Our long-serving chairman, Derek Schove, died in 1986 and was succeeded at first by William Page (now our President) and latterly local schoolmaster Martin Light.

After forty years in Beckenham Library our meeting place moved about a hundred yards further east along the Beckenham Road to the Day Centre at the junction with Hayne Road, but the Branch continues to flourish and attracts excellent attendances at all its gatherings.

Introduction

Recently I came across a folder full of old family photographs. Some of the pictures had notes on the back, and there was my mother wearing a wide hat and even wider skirt, standing on skis on the top of an Alp in 1911. But many of the pictures were unmarked and unrecognisable. Was that woman wearing a Victorian bonnet and standing next to the rather earnest-looking middle-aged man holding a bowler hat Great Aunt Jemima? And was that Great Uncle William or possibly Cousin Frederick? There was no way of knowing, there were no notes, everyone who might have remembered them was dead – and so the pictures have lost much of their value and their meaning.

A good local history can be as valuable and enjoyable as an old, well-kept family photograph album. It reminds us of the changing face and the changing shape of our surroundings, and this Anthology edited by Doris Pullen and John Wagstaff provides many descriptions of old scenes and early habits which are all too easy to forget.

In the last century local historians were faced with a shortage of accessible records, but the scene that they sought to record changed slowly over the years. Since the middle of the nineteenth century, however, life in Beckenham has changed at an accelerating pace, and it is all the more important that skilled observers such as H. Rob Copeland should record the changing scene before it is buried under mounds of paper in dusty files.

Sir Philip Goodhart, MP

1984

Village Place, Beckenham 1838 (permission: Bromley Library Service)

Graham Smith

Beckenham's Forefathers

The Parish of Beckenham once extended from the north at Stumps Hill, in Southend Road, to West Wickham in the south, to near what is now Bromley South Station in the east, and to the Crystal Palace in the west. It was in the Hundred of Bromley and the Lathe of Sutton at Hone, in the Sevenoaks Parliamentary Division of Kent, and the Rural Deanery of Beckenham, in the Diocese of Rochester. In the Domesday Book the name appears as 'Bacheham', and in *Textus Roffensis* – a collection of ancient charters, compiled by Bishop Ernulphus – it is 'Becceham', or the 'town of beeches'. Bacheham was once held by a Saxon, Ansgotus, under Odo, the Bishop of Bayeux.

A wooden church possibly existed at Beckenham even before the Conquest, as in *Textus Roffensis (1115-1125)* it is said that 'Becceham paid 9d a year Chrism rent' to the Mother Church of the Diocese. 'Chrism rent' was a yearly fee paid by the Parish priest for the consecrated oils used in the administration of the sacraments. Beckenham Church appears in the Taxation of Pope Nicholas IV, so a

Flooding at Beckenham High Street after heavy rain, April 1878 (permission: H.R. Copeland)

village community may have been there even then, and in the reign of
Queen Matilda a Charter of 1141 refers to a place known as 'Bekaham'.

In *Beckenham Past and Present* (1910), Robert Borrowman writes
that 'John de Malmains obtained a charter for the preservation or
custody of beasts and fowls in his lands at Beggenham from Edward II in
1318'. A descendant of de Malmains held 'twelve plough lands' or a
'knight's fee', which is as much land as could be reasonably ploughed in
a year by twelve ploughs. The owner of a 'knight's fee' had to attend the
lord on horseback, armed as a knight, for forty days each year, and this
was counted as rent for the lands that he held.

Jack Cade, who in 1450 led a revolt of Kentish men who marched on
London in protest against heavy taxation, obtained some of his rebels
from the parish of Beckenham. Robert and Richard Langley, and the
Constable of Beckenham, Robert Payne, are mentioned in the book
Illustrations of Jack Cade's Rebellion, by B.B. Orridge, FGS and W.D.
Cooper, FSA (published in 1869).

During the reign of Edward I, the Manor of Beckenham was held by
the De la Rochelle family from France. From Isolda, daughter of Philip
de la Rochelle and wife of Sir William Bruyn (or Le Bruin), the Manor
passed through her descendants to Sir Henry Bruin, who died in the
reign of Henry VI. His daughter Elizabeth was the mother of Sir
Charles Brandon, Duke of Suffolk, who is said to have lived for a while
in Beckenham Manor and entertained Henry VIII as he passed through
during his journeys to visit Anne Boleyn at Hever Castle. Another
daughter, Alice, had three husbands, the last being William Berners.
Their son John Berners inherited part of the land on the death of his
mother, and afterwards it passed from him to the Leigh family, who
alienated it to Henry Snelgrove.

After Elizabeth Brandon died part of the inheritance passed through
several hands, ultimately coming into the possession of Sir George
Dalston of Cumberland in the reign of Charles I: Sir George sold out to
Patrick Curwen.

Sir Oliver St John of Battersea bought this land and, after his death,
his son Walter St John became the new owner of the Bruin estates.
Eventually the land passed from Baron St John of Battersea to his son
Viscount Bolingbroke in 1742. The latter was succeeded by his nephew
Frederick, who in 1773 sold the manor to John Cator, the originator of
the vast Cator estate.

John Cator built Beckenham Place, circa 1780, as his new residence
and disposed of the old Manor House to the Burrell family. Beckenham
Place now serves in part as the club-house of the municipal golf-course
(actually owned by the London Borough of Lewisham rather than
Bromley) in Beckenham Place Park. In 1985 Beckenham Place is
expected to become the permanent home of an enormous collection of
theatrical memorabilia built up over many years by Joe Mitchenson,
who once lived in nearby Sydenham, and the late Raymond Mander.

Beckenham Place Park, circa 1960
(permission: M.V. Searle)

In 1788 Peter Burrell IV sold the Manor House to the Hoares, the banking family, who were related to him by marriage. The old Manor House later became what is now the Old Council Hall in Bromley Road.

Detailed information about the history of the other Manors of Beckenham – Kelsey, Langley and Foxgrove – can be found in H. Rob Copeland's *The Manors of Old Beckenham* (1967). Other recommended reading includes:

Robert Borrowman, *Beckenham Past and Present* (1910)
H. Rob Copeland, *The Village of Old Beckenham* (first published 1962)
Constance A.N. Trollope, *Beckenham in the Olden Times, 1538-1660* (1898)
G.W. Tookey, an article on Kelsey Park (1975)
Supplement to the *Beckenham Journal* on local history (1936)
Introduction to the History of Beckenham prepared by the staff of Beckenham Library (which has in its archives an excellent collection of local history material)

Charter Day, September 26th, 1935

PROGRAMME

of

Charter Ceremony
and Celebrations

. .
.

KINDLY NOTE

(1) For the benefit of the public, microphones and loudspeaker apparatus will be provided in connection with the proceedings on the Town Hall Balcony and on the Platform in the Recreation Ground.

(2) If the weather be definitely wet the actual presentation ceremony will be held, by very kind permission of the Directors, in the Regal Cinema in lieu of the Recreation Ground. In that event it is likely that much of the space will be occupied by guests and the school-children, and limited accommodation be available for the public. May the day be one of sunshine!

(3) One expects that the good folk of Beckenham will rally in large numbers as witnesses of this historic ceremony. Orderly and smooth working contribute much to the success of such an occasion. It is confidently hoped that all present will readily respond to the directions or requests of police, traffic-controllers and stewards.

We have to go early to press and gather, at time of printing, that the official arrangements are not complete in all respects.

We have been furnished, however, with the following provisional outline of the Order of Ceremony, which may be subject to variation and amplification.

49

Page from the Official Handbook of the Charter Celebrations, 1935 (permission: H.R. Copeland)

'Beckenham has Grown Up':
The Charter of Incorporation

The period between the World Wars saw a major transformation in many of the outlying parts of London. Just beyond the north of the metropolis, little-known villages like Cockfosters and Oakwood were becoming suburbs almost overnight in the wake of Underground Railway expansion: indeed, the railway companies even had to invent some names, such as Queensbury (near Kingsbury), to identify what had hitherto been 'virgin territory'.

In Beckenham the change was less dramatic. As the previous chapter indicated, a settlement has existed here since before the Norman Conquest, and it was the advent of surburban steam railways in the 1860s which caused a sudden boost to the size of the population. The only railway in the locality which in its early years failed to attract a significant population growth along its route was the section between Elmers End and Hayes of the so-called Mid-Kent Line, opened in 1882. Over this portion speculative development remained virtually non-existent until the eventual electrification of the line in 1925.

Immediately afterwards, however, the population of Eden Park and West Wickham began to rise sharply, with rows of very affordable semi-detached houses springing up along and in the vicinity of the Upper Elmers Road and, in many cases, noticeably superior housing appearing in West Wickham and on a spacious estate at Park Langley. As a result of West Wickham's enormous population growth, in April 1934 it was brought within the auspices of the Beckenham Urban District Council.

This 'stroke of a pen' enlargement of Beckenham's official area brought the total population of the town – it could hardly henceforth be termed a village – to over 67,000. Under the terms of the Municipal Corporations Act of 1882, as modified by the Local Government Acts of 1888 and 1933, Beckenham was thus now entitled to shed its humble UDC status and, by virtue of being granted a Charter of Incorporation, call itself a Borough. And from the lately-built Town Hall, near the junction of the High Street and Bromley Road, would emanate a Mayor, Aldermen, Burgesses and all the other trappings flowing from a Charter of Incorporation bestowed by Royal Prerogative.

Even though in purely practical terms the granting of Borough, or Corporation, standing was to be little more than a status symbol, it nevertheless took some months to complete the legal niceties of transition from Urban District Council to Municipal Borough (still, of course, within the County of Kent). But the elevation gave Beckenham

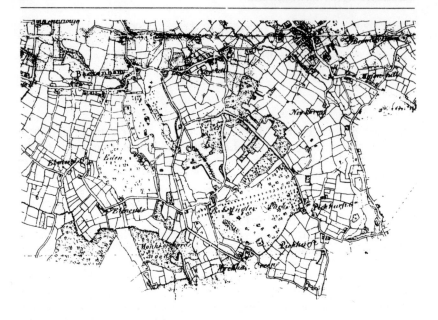

tangible superiority over, for example, neighbouring Penge, which was destined to remain a mere Urban District Council for a further thirty years. Such, indeed, was the sense of civic pride that an elaborate programme of celebrations was organised to coincide with Charter Day – Thursday, 26 September 1935.

That morning the Lord Mayor of London, Sir Stephen Killik, and his distinguished party swept into the new Borough of Beckenham – from the West Wickham direction, which was symbolic rather than geographically expedient – and the very first Mayor of Beckenham, Sir Josiah Stamp, was ceremonially presented with the Charter of Incorporation before appreciative crowds at the Croydon Road Recreation Ground. After the singing of the hymn *Now thank we all our God* and a dedicatory prayer by the Lord Bishop of Rochester, the procession made its way through the High Street to the Public Hall.

During the afternoon the excitement at Croydon Road was maintained by a funfair, followed in the evening by open-air dancing to 'Mr. Petchey's Orchestra'. For those who could run to three shillings for a ticket ('including light refreshments'), a more formal affair on offer as an alternative was a Gala Dance at the nearby Regal Ballroom. Then again, for revellers seeking a more sedate manner in which to celebrate the events of the day, a Whist Drive was held at the West Beckenham Hall in Sidney Road. Price of admission here was two shillings and if that was too much – well, there was the 'Entertainment of Beckenham Cine-Sound Productions' at a modest threepence.

Continuing attractions the following day included Music in Kelsey Park – with flood-lighting and illuminations at dusk – and a carnival dance at the Eden Park Hotel. Finally, on Saturday, 28 September the festivities concluded with Sports at the Croydon Road Recreation Ground, the 'Metrogas' Band playing in the Blake Recreation Ground at West Wickham, and a display at Croydon Road by the Women's League of Health and Beauty.

Edwin Davies, editor of the Charter Handbook which was widely available in September 1935 and of which copies must still repose in scores of Beckenham households, writes in his introduction, 'Beckenham has grown up. The district which not so many years ago was but a series of scattered hamlets...has grown to a big town, the second largest in Kent...'.

Davies was not to visualise that a mere generation later, in April 1965, Beckenham itself was to be swallowed up by the new London Borough of Bromley, the status of which may undergo further change in the event of the abolition of the Greater London Council.

So progress marches on – and little can be done to stop it. But, with the dedicated endeavours of the local historian, the present (which so soon becomes the past) can be recorded. Memories of the Charter of Incorporation – and indeed something of the community spirit which prevailed in Beckenham half a century ago – are kept not only by the written word of the Handbook and local newspapers. Broomfield Road resident Mr John Mantle and his friends at the Beckenham Cine Society made, in 1935, a delightful amateur film about 'Greater Beckenham' which is still shown to interested audiences.

Two Moated Sites In Beckenham

There are two known moated sites in Beckenham (Foxgrove and Elmers End), five more elsewhere in the London Borough of Bromley (Scadbury, Simpson's Place, Bromley Palace, Aperfield and Bertray's), about two hundred in Kent as a whole and of the order of 5,000 in England. Other moated sites close by include Eltham, Crayford, Crockenhill and Sutton-at-Hone, as well as a string along the Darent Valley.

Moats are usually associated with castles, but these were the exception rather than the rule and most were dug around Manor Houses

Foxgrove Farm and Moat (taken from 1871 map and superimposed on modern street plan, scale 1/3)

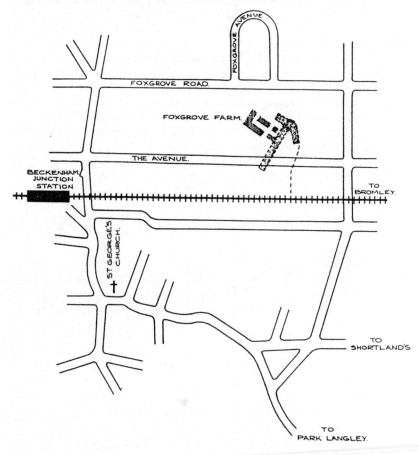

or large farms to give a measure of protection to the farmer and his family, as well as to his stock, from bands of thieves. Many sites which are now moated were first occupied prior to the Conquest, with the most popular time for building a defensive moat being between 1250 and 1350. There are now no visible signs of either of the two Beckenham moated sites, but we do have a reasonable level of information about their history.

Foxgrove Manor or Farm stood between Foxgrove Road and the Avenue (which used to be called Moat Road) as shown on the map. This was prepared from a map of 1871 superimposed on the modern street plan. The cross hatched area shows farm buildings at that time, whilst the shaded area shows the remains of the moat. There was no trace at that time of the west and south arms and only a portion of the northern, although there was an extension on the east side. Such extensions were, however, not uncommon.

The early history of Foxgrove is not clear, but a John de Foxgrove is recorded in about 1350. The estate passed through many hands over the years and in the late 1700s was acquired by the Burrell family, who incidentally also owned Simpson's Place in Bromley. The old manor house was demolished about 1830 and a new farm-house built on the site. This was pulled down about 1878, but the moat was not drained until some years later.

An attractive photograph of the farm house and the eastern arm of the moat is included in H.R. Copeland's *The Manors of Old Beckenham*. John Rocque's map of 1741-45 appears to show a four-sided moat but it is not entirely clear, and certainly by 1871 it had been reduced to the 'T' shape shown. Towards the end of the last century the West Kent Drainage Scheme tapped the stream which fed the moat. This had the effect of drying out the site, eventually leading to its being filled in. Whilst no visible signs remain, some of the local residents (who were totally unaware that a moat had existed in the area) report that water lies in parts of their gardens after heavy rain.

Elmers End site lies about 400 yards north west of Elmers End Station on the now derelict land which until the 1960s was used as a sewage farm. As with Foxgrove and many other historic sites, little is known of the early history, but there is evidence pointing to a Lord Robert de Retford as being the owner in about 1300, although that name is not mentioned in the Rolls of 1334-5. The land surrounding the moated house was for some reason limited to about twenty acres, and interestingly it was just off and apparently not connected to the track which ran from Beckenham to Croydon. The site is flat and low lying and just below the hills rising to Anerley and Crystal Palace. It is now drained by two small streams, but this may have been different at the time when the moat was built. Dr D.J. Schove has shown that the period 1310-20 was exceptionally wet, and it may be that the house was damaged and then demolished as a result of continuous flooding.

The Elmers End site is unusual in that it consisted of two concentric moats. These are shown on a number of maps and were excavated in the mid-1970s. The outer moat was dug at a slightly later date than the inner one; this may have been to assist drainage during the period of wet weather and flooding in the early 1300s. The excavations revealed thirteenth and fourteenth century pottery, building stone, and base frame for a bridge and other timbers, some of which may have been used for shoring the moat sides.

Thos. Motley's estate map of 1736 clearly shows the concentric moats, which incidentally are referred to as 'La Motes' The map makes no mention of an adjacent or connected house. A deed of 1467 (see *Archaeologia Cantiana*, 1975, Vol. 91, article by Lilian Thornhill, also Calendar of Deeds in Beckenham Library, ref B8 091(A)) refers to the area as Leweland and mentions 'gardens and motes', whilst a deed of 1494 refers to the 'Lewmote'. A map of 1723 of Peter Burrell's estates (i.e. only thirteen years before Motley's map) refers to the area as 'Lame Oats' and does not show the moat at all, but it does show the immediate area as being wooded.

The area was bought in the 1860s by the Croydon Board of Health and the moated part levelled. It was then used as a sewage farm and abandoned in the 1960s. Early Ordnance Survey (OS) maps and the excavations indicate that the central mound had an area of about 0.22 acres (80 ft x 120 ft). Both the inner and outer moats were about twenty feet wide and the bank between the two, about 45 feet wide. The concentric feature was certainly unusual, but otherwise the area of the central mound was on the small side, as was the width of the moats.

Beckenham's Churches

Chapter two explained how the coming of suburban railways to Beckenham in the 1860s led to a spectacular growth of population. In 1861 the population of the village was 2,391; in 1871 it was 6,090, in 1881 13,011 and by 1891 29,707. A soaring population meant expanding spiritual requirements, and this was in turn reflected by a mushrooming of places to worship.

Prior to 1864 there was only one church in the village, the Parish Church of St George, the development of which is dealt with in detail in Robert Borrowman's *A short description of the Parish Church of Beckenham*, published in 1906. With the development of the Cator Estate, it had been proposed to build houses and shops in the New Beckenham area, on both sides of the railway, but the plans did not fully mature although a church was erected in that area. St Paul's Church, a daughter church of St George's, was built in 1864, consisting of the Nave and North Porch. In 1872 a separate Parish was created when the main church was consecrated.

The next church to be built, at the other end of the village, was St Mary's, Shortlands. The foundation stone was laid on 5 October 1867 and the church opened in July 1868. In 1870 Shortlands was formed into an ecclesiastical district, out of the mother church, and the first part of the church was consecrated on 21 December of that year. In 1888 the enlarged building was consecrated, together with the organ. The church and lych-gate were entirely destroyed during World War Two, and the present church was consecrated in 1955.

The history of Christ Church, Beckenham, began in 1873 when a temporary iron church was built in The Avenue, Beckenham, to relieve pressure on the accommodation offered by the Parish Church. The foundation stones for the church in Fairfield Road were laid in April 1875 by the Earl of Shaftesbury, and the church was consecrated on 20 May 1876. In 1930 a Carillon of hand-operated bells was given in memory of the Rev Dr Harrington Lees, a former vicar of the church and later Archbishop of Melbourne, Australia. The church was severely damaged by a flying bomb in 1944 and, after re-building, was re-hallowed in 1950.

The Old Beckenham Mission, in Bromley Road, built in 1876, was founded by Mr B.A. Heywood of 'Banner', Westgate Road, and by Captain P.W. Stephens. John Hooker, Churchwarden at Christ Church, was associated with the Mission, and when he died Mr George Gatton was appointed Missioner.

*St George's Church, Beckenham, prior to reconstruction, 1885
(permission: Bromley Library Service)*

In 1877 the first Congregational services in Beckenham were started
by a group of people in an iron room at New Beckenham Station. A
lecture hall was built in Oakhill Road and opened on 30 July 1878.

In the same year two more churches were built; Holy Trinity,
Lennard Road and St Barnabas in Oakhill Road, the latter having been
a separate parish since 1877. The building of this church was carried out
in stages, the whole being completed in 1933. Like many other churches
the building was badly damaged by bombs in 1944, but was restored in
1948. St Peter's Hall, in Malmains Way, Park Langley, was built in 1954
to serve that part of the Parish.

St James's Church, Elmers End, was built in 1879, at first as a Chapel
of Ease to the Parish Church, but a separate parish was created in 1924.
The original church was enlarged and dedicated on 29 April 1936.

With the continued growth in population, the Nonconformist
Churches began to be established. First, the Baptist Church in Elm
Road, where the foundation stones were laid in November 1882 and the
church formally opened in 1883; and two years later the Congregational
Mission Chapel in Langley Road, Elmers End.

Robert Borrowman in his book says: There was, in 1884, considerable activity on the part of Nonconformists in Beckenham, for at that time the Wesleyan body first started their services by meeting in the Public Hall, Bromley Road; and on 3 September the memorial stones of a Congregational Mission Chapel in Langley Road were laid, and four memorial stones of the Wesleyan Chapel, in Bromley Road, were laid and the church building opened on 28 September of the same year. (Incidentally, these memorial stones have never been traced, and may lie below the present ground level.) Also in 1887 building work started on the Congregational Church , in Crescent Road, but the church was not opened until June 1888.

The St Augustine's Mission Hall, in Churchfields Road, was opened in 1886, and in 1910 a dual purpose Hall and Church was started, the present church being consecrated on 31 May 1945.

In 1891 the first Roman Catholic Church (now demolished) was built in Overbury Avenue. Two years later the Arthur Road Mission in Churchfields Road was opened. The Church of St Michael and All Angels in Birkbeck Road was begun in 1899, but it was not opened until 1906. After being destroyed by fire during the last war, a new church was built facing Ravenscroft Road, and was consecrated on 7 October 1956.

In 1907 two small churches were opened at Clock House. All Saints, which stood at the junction of Clock House Bridge and Chaffinch Road, was a Mission Church of St Augustine's and was removed when St Augustine's was created a separate parish. The other was the Wesleyan Chapel in Clock House Road. The Congregational Free Church in Goddard Road was built in 1931, incorporating the Mission Hall in Langley Road.

Reverting to 1907, Christ Church Mission Room was established in Croydon Road, between the Cottage Hospital and Shaftesbury Road, and it was the worshippers at the Mission who formed the nucleus of the congregation for the new church of St John's at Eden Park. The iron hut of the Mission was transported to Eden Park Avenue and was used for worship until the present church was built; it was consecrated in 1936.

The Catholic Convent of Handmaids of the Sacred Heart was founded in Foxgrove Road in 1930, and a new chapel opened in September 1936. St Edmund's Catholic Church in Village Way was founded in 1933 and the present church dedicated in 1938.

Two evangelistic churches complete the picture of churches in Beckenham, the Evangelical Church at The Hall in Cromwell Road, and the Christian Witness Church in Rectory Road.

The Beckenham Parochial Charities

The Beckenham Parochial Charities is a charitable body, controlled by the Charity Commissioners, which exists mainly to administer the Anthony Rawlins Almshouses for Widows at numbers 1, 3 and 5 Bromley Road, adjacent to the Beckenham Parish Church and dating from 1694. The Parochial Charities also own the property at 31 and 33 Bromley Road, known as the Bertie Cator Almshouses. These were built in 1890 in memory of Peter Cator (seventh son of Joseph Cator and Diana Bertie of Clock House) by his widow of The Hall, Bromley Road. They were originally controlled by her estate, then taken over by the London Borough of Bromley, and finally, after reconstruction, by the Beckenham Parochial Charities. The Anthony Rawlins Almshouses are for widows who have lived for at least three years in the area of the former Beckenham Urban District Council, but the Bertie Cator Almshouses have no such restrictions and may be occupied by widows, spinsters, widowers or bachelors.

The Charities have their origins in eight constituent bodies which were founded at various dates between 1674 and 1925. They are:

1   The Charities of Edmund Style and others, founded 1674
2   The Charity known as Anthony Rawlins Almshouses, founded 1694
3   The Beckenham Parochial Educational Fund, founded 1790
4   The Charity of Mrs Mary Watson, founded about 1790
5   The Charity of Mary Wragg, founded about 1799
6   The Charity of William Fenner, founded about 1807
7   The Charity of Elizabeth Ann, Dowager Duchess of Exeter, founded 1837
8   The Randell Memorial Fund, founded 1925.

The present revised scheme for their joint administration was sealed by Order of the Charity Commissioners on 10 July 1978, following extensive correspondence and meetings under the chairmanship of the late Hugh F. Burgess. Naturally, however, this local organisation goes back much further, the first Scheme being dated 9 September 1880. Prior to that the various Charities had been under the control of the St George's Parochial Church Council.

The present Trustees are: one ex-officio trustee, the Rector for the time being of the Ecclesiastical Parish of St George, Beckenham; six nominative trustees (people who through residence, occupation or employment, or otherwise have special knowledge of the area and who are appointed by the Council of the London Borough of Bromley); four co-optive trustees (people who through residence, occupation or employment, or otherwise have special knowledge of the Ancient Parish

The Anthony Rawlins Alshouses for Widows, 1–5 Bromley Road, 1982 (permission: M.V. Searle)

of Beckenham and are appointed by the Trustees themselves). All appointments are for five years. Meetings are usually held quarterly.

Apart from the Almshouses, the Charities are invested in land in Oakwood Avenue, and in investments standing in the name of the Official Custodian for Charities. The Educational Fund is primarily for the purpose of advancing education for young people under the age of eighteen resident, or attending school, in or near the area of the Ancient Parish of Beckenham, who are in need of financial assistance. The Randell Memorial Fund is similarly available for the acquisition of personal sports equipment, in particular for local children in need.

Some Beckenham Schools

The Village School, Bromley Road

The Infants' School in Bromley Road has been in constant use as a place of education since 1818. In 1811 a National Society had been formed 'for promoting the Education of the Poor in the principles of the Established Church', and in 1818 it was decided to form a branch in Beckenham Parish and to provide a school. The site was a field adjoining the church, given by the Lord of the Manor, John B. Cator, and the school was opened in 1818 with 36 boys and 36 girls, mostly children whose parents worked on local estates.

The school consisted of two classrooms, one for boys and one for girls, with a house in between for the Master. The first Master was Thomas Pritchett, and his eldest daughter acted as Mistress for the girls. Part of the ground floor of the Master's house still exists, in the building facing Bromley Road, and the two original classrooms are still in use today for the purpose for which they were built. The original door by which the first children entered can still be seen in one of these rooms.

The extensions to the school building carried out in 1906 produced the accommodation which is still familiar today, as only alterations and improvements such as central heating and indoor toilets have been carried out since. In 1907 the girls' school accommodation was for 296, but this did not prevent there being 338 on the books in 1909. In fact throughout the years this school has been in existence it has nearly always been very well attended, and only such catastrophes as the war-time bombing and the 1944 evacuation of school children from Beckenham have reduced the roll below the level of accommodation.

St James's School and the Marian Vian Schools, Elmers End

In 1879 the hamlet of Elmers End was a farming community of a few hundred people, with no school, and only a small iron-built church to serve them, but in that year a plot of land was given for the erection of a new church and school in a position accessible to the community. No time was lost, the buildings were erected and paid for by public subscription, and St James's school was opened in 1880. The school was behind the church, set among fields with a little stream running through them and with a line of stately elm trees, under which lessons could be taken in summer. But with the rapid growth of Elmers End district after the first war, and the building of council estates, the little school could not accommodate all the children of the neighbourhood and the erection of two Council Schools was set in hand. These schools were to be named the Marian Vian Schools, after the lady of that name, who had devoted so much of her time to local education. She was a member of the Education Committee, a JP, and a governor of several schools. She died in 1934, but in 1948 the schools were visited by her nephew, Admiral Sir Philip Vian, renowned in the Second World War for his command of the *Cossack* which rescued 299 British seamen from the German ship *Altmark*, and immortalised it in the famous words 'The Navy's Here'.

On 8 January 1930, some 176 children assembled at St James's school and, with each one carrying a little bundle of books tied up with string, marched across to the new school in Adams Road. (This has lately been renamed Kingsworth Close.) In May 1930, St James's school was permanently closed and the last 158 children, of senior age, became pupils at Marian Vian Secondary School. Most of the buildings comprising St James's school are still in use as church premises, though parts were demolished when the church was extended in 1935. The green fields and the play area however have disappeared under streets of houses, and the elm trees were felled to make room for the church extension.

In 1932 the infants were separated from the juniors, and moved into the newly completed building in Shirley Crescent, making three schools each under its own Head. The Secondary School became a Girls' school in the reorganisation after the War; later it became a mixed school known as Spring Park Lower, and was finally closed in July 1979. Owing to falling rolls, the junior and infants' two schools have, in 1983, been merged into a single unit, which continues to flourish.

Beckenham County Grammar School for Girls, Lennard Road, and the Beckenham Central Schools, Balgowan Road

The County Councils, which took over responsibility for the running of schools from the school boards in 1904, were empowered to provide education of a higher standard for pupils who could benefit from it, and two schools were planned and built, one for girls in Lennard Road, and one with separate departments for boys and girls in Balgowan Road. The one in Lennard Road was to become the Beckenham County Grammar School for Girls, and the one in Balgowan Road became the Boys' and Girls' Central Schools. There was later a separate Infants school on this same site.

Before either of these schools was ready for use, the Great War had started, and both buildings were requisitioned and used as hospitals. To the present day, both schools display the certificate of thanks for their use issued in 1919 by the Army Council. In addition, Balgowan school has two other momentoes. In the hall is a plaque listing the fact that

5,257 soldiers were treated there between 1915 and 1919, and adding that the doctors and nurses were assisted by two companies of Kent VAD.

The other reminder is a book, which was given to the headmaster recently by an elderly man who had been one of those patients in 1916. Apparently every man treated at the hospital was presented with *The Queen's Gift Book*, which was sold in aid of Queen Mary's Auxiliary Hospitals Charity.

In 1919 both buildings were opened for the purpose for which they had been built, and they became flourishing schools. The County Grammar School was extended in 1927, and in 1959 it moved to new premises on a new site in Eden Park. In 1973 it became a comprehensive school taking girls of all abilities, and the name was changed to Langley Park Girls' School. The school badge incorporates the arms of the Style family who lived at Langley Park for some 200 years. The Balgowan Schools, separately organised for boys and girls, took children who had just failed to qualify for a place at a Grammar school, and were known as Central schools. Upon the reorganisation of the Borough schools at the end of the 1940s, the Central Schools as such ceased to exist and the boys school was closed, but Balgowan Girls', extended by taking the girls from Bromley Road and other schools, continued on the same site as a Secondary Modern School until 1959. Then the girls moved to the buildings vacated by the Grammar School in Lennard Road, and renamed Cator Park School for Girls. The school became fully comprehensive in the late 1970s.

When the Secondary school left the Balgowan buildings they were turned over to Primary school use, and soon established their mark as flourishing Junior and Infants schools serving the neighbourhood between Croydon Road and Clockhouse and even beyond.

Boys' Schools

Mention has already been made of the fact that the original Beckenham School was built for boys and girls. It cannot now be ascertained when boys over 11 ceased to go there, but it was before the Second World War. In 1889 the need for a school at the other end of the Parish had become urgent, and some Church land was sold by the trustees to the Beckenham School Board for £900, for the erection of a building, first called Arthur Road School, but later renamed Churchfields School, both the name and the building being still in use. It was opened for children of all ages in 1890, and was extended in 1907. It is now a Primary school, and the proposal to rebuild it on the nearby allotment site has in 1983 been much in the news, and has given rise to great controversy.

After the Local Government Act of 1888, the Local School Boards were allowed to spend money on Secondary education, and it was

decided to build a Technical Institute. This is the building next to the
Baths, on the site of the old Clock House, and the foundation stone
dated 25.7.1899 is on the front, and carved in stone on the side, the
words 'Science' and 'Art'. The school was opened in 1901.

In 1931 the boys moved to a new purpose-built building in Penge High
Street, and became Beckenham and Penge Grammar School, and the
Institute building then housed a Junior Technical School, for which boys
were selected at the age of 13. This school was closed in 1958, when the
boys were transferred to the new Technical School at Keston. The
building has since then been used for adult education.

The Grammar School in the High Street went from strength to
strength, and made a name for itself in the district and beyond, but then
was moved, in 1968, again to new premises, and has become Langley
Park Boys' School. It now, like the Girls' school, takes children of all
abilities.

In 1900 a school was opened in Parish Lane to serve the Penge end of
Beckenham, and to relieve the pressure on Beckenham Parish school.
This was the Alexandra School, and of course then took children of all
ages. In 1929 a new school for the Infants was opened in Kent House
Road, and in 1954 the Junior school moved to new buildings in Cator
Road. Both these schools still bear the name Alexandra. By this time
the Secondary school took only boys, but under the post war
reorganisation it was closed in April 1968 upon the opening of the new
Kelsey Park School, to which the boys were transferred. The Victorian
building was then demolished, and upon the site has been erected the
Anne Sutherland accommodation for the elderly. One of the original
gateposts and one boundary wall are all that now remains of the old
school.

When the Grammar School vacated the Penge High Street building, a
new school for boys took over the premises, and is known as Kentwood.

Private Schools

There are only a few private schools existing now in Beckenham,
although in the past there have been many more, both for boys and
girls.

St Christopher's Girls' School in Bromley Road, occupies a house long
known as The Hall which was owned and lived in by members of the
Cator family. In 1893 a school called The Hall was started there. In the
same year, a school called St Christopher's was opened in Perth Road,
and after moving twice from there, in 1926 it moved to The Hall, the
two schools became one, and there it has remained ever since. In recent
years much building work has been carried out in the grounds, and it is
now a flourishing independent day school taking girls from 3-18 years,
and boys from 3-8 years.

St Christopher's School, Bromley Road, circa 1910: Enid Blyton (with pigtail), third from right, middle row (see page 43)

Beckenham Convent in Westgate Road, is a school run by nuns of the Convent of the Handmaids of the Sacred Heart of Jesus, an order founded in Spain, but now with schools in many countries. The Beckenham Convent, which occupies a large corner site in Westgate and Foxgrove Roads, opened in 1930, for girls of all ages. In 1968 a new Primary School, known as St Mary's, was built on part of the grounds. This is classified as a Voluntary Aided Primary School under Bromley Education Committee, and takes boys and girls up to the age of 11. The Convent School, which is entirely independent, now only takes girls of secondary school age, of whom about a quarter are boarders.

Eden Park School, occupies a site and a house in Upper Elmers End Road formerly called The Hollies. It was founded in the mid 1930s by Mrs A. Mallick, who ran it until her death. It educates boys and girls from 4-11 years.

St David's College, is now partly in West Wickham, but it was founded in 1926 at 29 South Eden Park Road, Beckenham, as a Junior School for boys and girls. The first Principal was Mrs G. Davies, who adopted the then-fashionable term College. The present Headmaster is Dr. D.J. Schove, Chairman of the Beckenham Historical Association, which holds occasional meetings at the main building at Justin Hall. The grounds still connect the Hall with 'Number 29', and the whole site was part of Lord Gwydir's estate, sold in 1820.

Former Private Schools

Woodbrook School: a school for girls and young boys known as Woodbrook flourished for many years in a large house in Hayne Road. When the school finally closed in 1960, the site was acquired by Beckenham Education Committee, who demolished the old house and erected a modern building which now houses one of the borough's special schools for handicapped children.

Minshull House School opened in Park Road in 1868 and took both day girls and boarders for 97 years, until it closed in 1965. The flats known as Minshull Court stand on its site.

In 1938 Miss A. Willsher founded the **Manor Preparatory School** which occupied two houses in Manor Road. It was most highly thought of in the district, taking girls up to 11 years, and boys from 5-7 years. Though the premises were not lavish, the school always had a waiting list, and at times rented rooms at Christ Church and the Methodist church in order to accommodate more children. One of the bank sports grounds was used for games, and the children were highly successful at swimming. There was sadness when this excellent school closed in 1971.

The largest and best known of the boys' schools was the **Abbey School** which was built on a beautiful site between Copers Cope and Park Roads. The land had been part of Copers Cope Farm, and the school was built in 1868 by the first headmaster Rev Thomas Lloyd Phillips and was aptly named, as the architecture was designed to give the impression of a venerable antique Abbey building. The school flourished and made a name for itself beyond the confines of Beckenham, but in 1940, to avoid the bombing, it moved to East Grinstead and never returned after the war. It finally closed in 1969.

The buildings had remained in partial use for various purposes for many years after the school left, but were finally demolished and the Abbey Estate of flats and houses has been built on the site. The Worsley Bridge Primary School was erected on the Abbey playing fields.

Clare House was a boys' Preparatory School in Oakwood Avenue, opened in 1896. It closed in 1970 and upon its site, Bromley Borough built the Primary school for boys and girls, which has retained the same name.

Craven College was a high class private school for boys at Elmer Lodge, Elmers End, a house which is still there and bears that name. As in all residential suburbs such as Beckenham, there have been other private schools, but of which no details are now available.

Acknowledgements: The Headmistress of Bromley Road Infants School for the loan of old Log Books
The Headmasters of Marian Vian and Balgowan Primary Schools
St James's Church Elmers End Centenary Booklet
The Headmistress of Cator Park Girls' School
Mr Allinson, Building and Sites Officer, Bromley Education Department

Beckenham Hospital

The second half of the nineteenth century saw many changes in attitude to the social problems of the time, not least in the care of the sick and poor. For Beckenham the numbers in need of such care had risen as a result of the rebuilding of the Crystal Palace and the construction of the many railways in the area. The idea of small cottage hospitals near to people's homes and open to fresh air had resulted in 74 such hospitals being established nationally between 1869 and 1885. Beckenham's Cottage Hospital was founded in 1872 by a group of local people who supported Mr Peter Richard Hoare of Kelsey Manor in his wish to provide at his own expense a building in Middle Barnet Field, Croydon Road to accommodate four beds in the care of a Matron and two honorary Medical Officers.

The first building was placed in the care of Trustees for five years at a rent of 1/- p.a. and Patients were charged 6d. per day. The first year resulted in a deficit of £77.10s.10d. but three years later eight beds were available and supported by a house to house collection. Before the five years were past, however, Peter Hoare died in 1877 and the trustees of

Beckenham Cottage Hospital, Croydon Road, circa 1872
(permission: H.R. Copeland)

his estate demanded a full rent of £80 p.a. – the first financial crisis in the life of the hospital. At the time the Beckenham Journal commented sadly that 'in a parish with many wealthy residents but a large proportion of artizans an institution like the hospital could languish for lack of funds'.

The situation was saved by the appointment of a full-time collector of funds. First a Mr Reed of Ravenscroft Road and then Mr Lawrence, a tobacconist on the Railway Bridge, who with his son successfully carried out the task from 1881 to 1917. So well did the public support the collectors that a Building fund was set up and in 1887 the freehold of the site was bought and a new wing added the following year.

The improvements overcame difficulties recorded in 1885 when it was said that eleven cases were being treated but with only eight beds the nurse and the servant had to give up their accommodation and that if a doctor attended a patient the others had to be moved into the kitchen! By 1891, however, the Staff consisted of a Matron, Nurse, a probationer and a cook plus a housemaid and a boy, with the number of beds increased to seventeen. A year later more than one hundred patients were admitted and it was reported that the hospital was becoming better known and appreciated by reference to the 'testimony of patients who had entered unwillingly but left with gratitude and contentment'.

As money became available so the hospital continued to develop. Queen Victoria's Jubilee years saw £1,500 raised towards the first children's ward and in 1903 a new operating theatre was built. In 1922 an appeal was launched for a major extension and the work was completed in 1926 at a cost of £32,000. By 1929 45 beds were available and fifteen per cent of patients treated without charge. Ten years later the Duchess of Gloucester opened further additions including the Trapnell Wing following an appeal for a million shillings.

With the outbreak of war in 1939, 125 beds were available and thousands of outpatients received treatment despite the loss of staff on active service. At the same time plans for further improvements and residential staff quarters were prepared but were delayed with the advent of the National Health Service. The major improvements were finally completed with the opening of Douglas Lindsey Ward in 1969.

Throughout the years prior to 1948, from Cottage to General Hospital, the community supported and developed a most valuable asset. Although the management now lies elsewhere as part of the NHS the strength of that support still exists in the community, and considerable financial aid is provided by local organisations and the Friends of the Hospital.

'Yes! I Remember It Well'.
A Walk Through the Village High Street

'I'm just going down to the Village' was a remark often heard in the early part of this century, for the High Street was the centre of village life, with shops and businesses serving the Manor Houses and Estates before the outlying areas such as Clock House, Elmers End, Eden Park and Park Langley were developed as shopping areas.

As a boy I walked every morning to school, through the High Street to Beckenham Road, home for dinner, back for afternoon lessons then home again for tea. I recall Squire Lea Wilson driving his coach-and-four down the Church Hill to his house opposite the end of Village Way, called Village Place, or The Cedars. I recall, too, the horse-buses and the changing of the horses a little further down the road; and sheep being driven through the High Street to the slaughter-house at the back of the shops, near the present Safeways store.

But let's start this walk at the beginning of the High Street and imagine ourselves back in the first decade of the twentieth century. At the Railway Station horse-cabs plied for hire on the down side of the station. Crossing the bridge we pass, on the left, the Railway Hotel, where a picture dated 1902 shows the last meeting of the West Kent Hounds. Near the hotel a floral rustic archway was erected to give

High Street, Beckenham, circa 1900
(permission: Bromley Library Services)

30

The George Inn, Beckenham

Clock House, Beckenham -

Beckenham Lodge

welcome to Princess Beatrice of Battenburgh who came, via Catford, to open an extension to the Cottage Hospital in 1899.

Passing the St George's Church Hall on the right, now St Bride's House, we come to the entrance gates of the Old Rectory, the foundation stone of which is built into one of the entrance lobbies of the Beckenham Town Hall, built in 1931.

Descending Church Hill we would see, on the top of an embankment to the right, a Gazebo which served as a look-out when the Squire's coach was expected back in the Village, and nearby The Cage, a temporary prison for drunks, the Stocks for miscreants, and the Pound for stray cattle.

Turning right at the foot of the hill we see, on the left, the River Beck passing as an open stream in front of the Greyhound Inn, where in the 1860s Dr R.R. Stilwell resided. Further along on the right, where now stands W.H. Smith's was the Old Wood House which, I believe, was once a Kentish Yeoman's Hall (the name given to a type of Kentish house built by medieval freeholders who farmed or grew their own hops), with Padbury's forge at the rear, one of several forges serving the Village horses; and Alcock the sadler nearby; opposite is the George Inn, dating back over 300 years.

Another very old building, on the left, was the Parish Clerk's house standing near to the present Safeways store. My grandfather's builders shop was on the site of the present Woolwich Building Society office, and in 1927 I took a photograph of my father standing in the old kitchen doorway among the demolition debris.

On the corner of Kelsey Square, where there is now a Greengrocer's Stall, was yet another very old building, the first meeting place of the Rural Sanitary Authority in 1872, with the fire station below. Between this building and 'The Three Tuns' was the old Police Station, while still further on was Austin's sausage shop, opened in the early 1850s and demolished in 1959, with chicken and sheep in its adjoining field.

On the other side of the road was a high brick wall enclosing Village Place, already referred to, now the parade of shops called Cedars

*Above: Garnham's Drapery Store, circa 1920
(permission both pictures: K. Walters)*

*Below: Garnham's after modernisation (and renumbering) shortly before
it closed in 1933*

*The Police Station, Beckenham High Street, 1982
(permission: M.V. Searle)*

Parade. The old building, once the residence of Col Samuel Wilson, Lord Mayor of London in 1838, was demolished in 1920 after being used for military purposes during the first world war.

The Pavilion cinema, opened in 1914 but demolished in the early 1930s, was on the corner of the High Street and Village Way; it seated about 400.

Another hundred yards or so, and our walk down the old Village High Street comes to an end opposite Beckenham Lodge, which stood behind the present Barclays Bank. Our second cinema, originally known as The Regal, seating about 2,000, and still in business as a triple-screen ABC, was built around 1930, about six years after the Rectory Estate had been developed.

In this limited article I have recalled only the outstanding buildings of the old Village High Street. Our readers will, no doubt, recall others, together with people and events which bring back to them memories of the Good Old Days.

The Wellcome Research Laboratories

Two young American pharmacists, Silas M. Burroughs and Henry S. Wellcome, formed a partnership (Burroughs Wellcome and Co.) in England in 1880 which became most successful. Burroughs died in 1895 and Wellcome took over the whole undertaking. This comprised commercial offices at Snow Hill in London, a chemical works at Dartford and the Wellcome Physiological Research Laboratories, originally in London, later at Brockwell Hall near Herne Hill and finally (from 1922) at its present abode at Langley Court, Beckenham.

This site had been part of the old estate of Langley, which had been established soon after the Norman Conquest when it was recorded in the Domesday Book as part of the vast possessions of Odo, Bishop of Bayeux and Earl of Kent. Over the years it belonged to the Malmains, Styles and Raymonds and was left (in 1768) by Jones Raymond to his sister Amy, widow of Peter Burrell of Kelsey. In 1820, the Langley estate (which extended from Monks Orchard in the South, beyond Elmers End to the West, to Beckenham High Street in the North and to Bromley in the East, a total of 3,202 acres) was sold in 92 lots. Langley Farm, comprising a residence (on the site of the present Langley Court Mansion), offices, coach-house, stables and entrance lodge on 249 acres 2 roods 31 perches was bought by the Goodhart family (no relation to the Member of Parliament) for £14,000. One of these buildings, a thatched cottage, thought by some to have been a chapel, still survives. If, as has been suggested, it is the chapel dedicated by the Bishop of Rochester in 1607, it is the oldest building in Beckenham. In 1884 Mr J.L. Bucknall, a shipping magnate, bought the farm and about half of its land from the Goodharts for £10,000, pulled down the farm and replaced it with the present Langley Court Mansion in 1886. Mr Wellcome bought the estate in 1920. Since then some of the land has been given to extend the sports field of Langley Park boys school and some to give drivers a better view round the bend in South Eden Park Road, and the estate now (1984) comprises 110 acres or 44 hectares.

The official name of the undertaking is 'The Wellcome Research Laboratories', but, in addition to the research (on both pharmaceuticals and biologicals), development and manufacture of vaccines and diagnostic reagents are carried out there. This causes the site to be designated a factory for the purposes of the Factories Act 1961 and associated legislation.

It is, however, for its research that the establishment is well-known throughout the world, and for the calibre of the scientists who have carried out that research. No fewer than ten members of the scientific staff have become Fellows of the Royal Society, the highest British scientific honour, three of these, Percival Hartley, J.H. Gaddum and

Early picture of Langley Court, now the offices of the Wellcome Foundation Laboratories, South Eden Park Road (permission: G. Pullen)

J.W. Trevan, after the laboratories moved to Beckenham. Several have achieved international honours, the most recent being the Nobel Prize by Dr J.R. Vane in 1982 for his work on prostaglandins.

A succession of improvements to vaccines, particularly for diptheria in the 1920s and 1930s by A.T. Glenny, Miss M. Barr and others, have contributed very significantly to the effectiveness and safety of present-day vaccines and resulted, for instance, in the virtual elimination of diptheria in this country.

Further examples of discoveries and developments of the Beckenham laboratories are:

1928-9 First dog distemper vaccine

1930 Digoxin isolated from digitalis (foxglove) leaves

1934 First antitoxin against lamb dysentery

1936 Yellow fever vaccine introduced

1938 Antibacterial effects of sulphone discovered

1938 Curare (with which natives used to tip their arrows to paralyse their enemies) purified for use as an anti-convulsant

1947 Cyclizine (anti-nauseant) and analgesics dipiparone and thiambutene discovered

1953 Development of egg-adapted dog distemper vaccine

1953 Triprolidine, the most potent anti-histamine, introduced

1959 Bretylium tosylate (adrenergic neurone blocking agent) introduced

1959 Bephenium, a new anthelmintic for humans and animals discovered

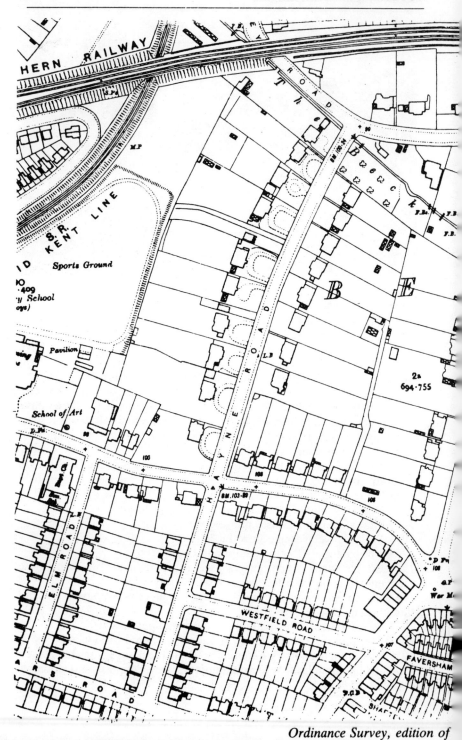

Ordinance Survey, edition of

1961 First 7-in-one sheep vaccine produced

1963 Anti-hypertensive, bethanidine sulphate discovered

1963 Development of a novel test for pregnancy

1971 First officially approved vaccine against Marek's disease (in poultry) introduced

1971 Rubella (German measles) vaccine, the first to be produced in the UK on human diploid cells (which minimises the risk of rejection/-reaction)

1971 First vaccine for the control of Foot Rot in sheep in UK

1975 A rapid test for Hepatitis B virus introduced

1976 Prostacyclin, which prevents the formation of blood clots in arteries, discovered

1977 A very rapid test to measure the level of digoxin in the blood developed

1978 Gletvax, a vaccine preventing the adhesion of coli bacteria to the gut wall, introduced

1980 The first large-scale supply of interferon for clinical evaluation in cancer therapy

1981 C. parvum vaccine developed

1981 Acyclovir, an anti-viral compound with unique action against herpes virus introduced.

The old thatched building referred to above is now used as an office by the Estate Manager. It has a clock made by Anthony Ireland of Mile End in about 1770. This still keeps good time and strikes the hours on a bell in a small turret. This bell is inscribed 'PETER BVRILL ESQr OF BECKNVM 1733' followed by four medallions which are so worn as to be indecipherable. The headstock is of wood and bears the date 1773. It is of the swinging variety but is now firmly fixed. Nowadays it is the hammer which strikes the stationary bell.

The variation in dates, it is suggested, may be explained in this way. The bell was made in 1733 for the cottage, as it probably was then, at the order of Peter Burrell Esq., one of the previous owners of the estate and well known in Beckenham historical circles, and installed then so that it could be tolled by a bell-ringer pulling a rope to swing the bell. In 1773 a new headstock was required and the present one was made. It was used for some time, for it bears the marks of use, and at some time later the clock was built into the loft, the same bell being immobilised and the hammer connected to the clock's striking train. This would make the most likely date for the clock some time not long after 1773.

In 1955 the flooring of the cottage was replaced by concrete, which required some excavation. During the digging an interesting coin was found about three inches below the surface of the soil. It was a halfpenny dated 1775 and issued in the reign of George III. Its diameter was 1.2 inches and depicted a laurate bust in armour on the obverse and Britannia seated, holding an olive branch in her right hand and a spear in her left on the reverse. The possibility of the coin having been dropped between the floorboards is ruled out by the depth at which it was found, for the ground had definitely been compressed to accommodate the weight of the floor and its occupants. The depth suggests that it was lost when the floor was originally installed, for although this had been patched from time to time, its joists had been laid many, many years ago.

Sources

Maxwell, G.S., *The Fringe of London*, 1931 chapter XV
Victoria County History of Kent
Hasted, *History of Kent*
Smith, J.R., *Bibliotheca Cantiana*
Lyson's Environs of London, Vol 2
Copeland, H.R., *From Village to Borough*
Tookey, G.W., *Kelsey, Langley and the Burrells*
Tookey, G.W., *The story of Park Langley*
Borrowman, R., *Beckenham Past and Present*

Personalities of Old Beckenham

The object of this publication is to bring to light hitherto unpublished material of local interest. In this chapter therefore, I shall not deal with people connected with our early history, nor personalities associated with the various estates of Beckenham Village.

In the records of early Chancery proceedings, during the reign of Henry IV, there is mention of litigation between Thomas Causton and William Causton with reference to lands situated in the 'towne and felds of Bekyham, in the shire of Kent'. Some historians believe that William Caxton lived in this district, but it is unlikely that this William Causton could have been William Caxton since the latter was born circa 1422, some nine years after Henry's death.

The followers in the Jack Cade Rebellion in 1450 included 22 men belonging to the Parish of Beckenham, among whom were Robert Langley, Richard Langley and Robert Pain, the last named being the Constable of Beckenham. This Richard Langley – or Langle – was probably the son of Ralph Langle of Beckenham who, in 1453, bequeathed three shillings and four pence towards the new bells in the Beckenham Parish Church; also money for 'amending the King's way between the Church and the Well in Bromley Road'.

There is a reference in 1750 to the death of John Cade, a well-known Kentish name, the Village Schoolmaster, and there is a tombstone to his memory in the Churchyard. A block of Council houses in the Upper Elmers End Road bears this name.

When we come to the twentieth century I am treading on dangerous ground for, although I was born in Beckenham and can recall many of the local personalities since the turn of the century, others may recall equally renowned names other than those mentioned below.

The Beckenham Urban District Council reflected local professions and trades, and many of those who gave their time to serve as Councillors have left their names in our recent history. William Lovelock had a stonemason's yard in the High Street, next to the Christ Church Hall. He supplied stonework for the re-built Kelsey Manor, and designed and donated the font in Christ Church. He was a member of the former Parochial Committee, afterwards the Local Board, and later still the Urban District Council. He was a Churchwarden of Christ Church.

The Revd Harrington Lees, Vicar of Christ Church early this century, became Archbishop of Melbourne, Australia, and the carillon of bells at Christ Church were installed in his memory.

Also in the High Street was a small wooden shop, built in the seventeenth century as a gardener's cottage for The Cedars opposite. Thomas Austin opened his shop there in the early 1850s for the making and selling of pork and beef sausages, and at the rear, he kept cows, sheep and chickens. Charlie Austin, his son, and two sisters were born there, and for over sixty years Charlie was a bellringer at the Parish Church.

The name of Padbury was well-known as a blacksmith and farrier, also as a coach-builder.

Early this century Vernon Chalk was the village butcher, with several meat and fish shops in the village. He kept a slaughter-house behind his High Street shop, opposite the present Woolworth's.

Nottle, the local photographer, meanwhile had premises near the old Railway Hotel, on the corner of Church Road, and many of his street photographs can still be seen in local exhibitions.

On the local Education Committee were Marian Vian, who lived in The Knoll; she is remembered in the Marian Vian School at Elmers End; as also is Revd Stewart Fleming, one-time Chairman of the Education Committee and for many years minister of the Elm Road Baptist Church, after whom the school in Witham Road is named.

Harry Lyne, our Village Postman, was, I believe, the first Labour Councillor on the local Urban District Council. He did much work for local charities, particularly the Cottage Hospital, where one of the wards bears his name. Another ward at the hospital bears the name of Stilwell. Dr R.R. Stilwell was, in the early 1860s, the only doctor in the Village, and his son George Stilwell and his grandson Denison were benefactors to the town.

Another well-known name in the High Street was Mr T.W. Thornton, who had a stationery and book shop at the bottom of Church Hill, with a printing works at the rear. Mr Thornton was a great public worker. Through his weekly newspaper, *The Beckenham Journal*, of which he became the proprietor in 1881 (the Journal having been formed five years earlier), he brought to the notice of local inhabitants issues of the day. It was through his efforts that the Local Council purchased Kelsey Park; and it was he who paid for the restoration of the twelfth-century Lych Gate at the Parish Church, in memory of two of his sons who died in the first World War. His youngest son, Victor, who worked for his father in the family business, was a great amateur actor and comedian.

A contemporary of Victor was Maurice Denham, whose father was a dentist in Albemarle Road. They were both members of the Beckenham Shakespeare Society in the 1920s.

Dr W.G. Grace, the famous cricketer, lived for a while in Beckenham and was buried in the Crystal Palace District Cemetery at Elmers End. A public house nearby is called the 'Dr W.G. Grace'. Enid Blyton the internationally known author of children's stories, lived as a child for several years from 1897 in Chaffinch Road, Beckenham. Educated at St Christopher's School, Bromley Road, she died in 1968.

Other celebrities who gave of their time in Local Government were Jack Bennett, House Agent and Coal Merchant of Clock House, who carried on the work of local history started by James Dennis and Robert Borrowman; he became an Alderman of the Beckenham Borough Council and later a County Alderman. Sir George Sutton, Chairman of the Urban District Council, with his wife did great work for the then Cottage Hospital, and a ward at the hospital bears the name of Ruth Sutton.

Mr C.A. Elgood, another Education Committee Chairman, gave his name to the former Elgood Playing Field where now stands the Kelsey Park Boys School.

Mr Archie Collister, son of John Collister who worked for a local builder, was the first Labour Councillor to be made Chairman of the Beckenham Urban Council.

More recently, when Beckenham obtained a Charter of Incorporation in 1935, Sir Josiah Stamp, later Baron Stamp of Shortlands, was elected Charter Mayor with Charles Eric Staddon as Charter Town Clerk, the Deputy Charter Mayors being Dr J.H. Bennett, and Alderman James Crease, after whom the park in Village Way was named. Lord and Lady Stamp, together with their eldest son Wilfrid Carlyle Stamp, were all killed at their home at Shortlands by a direct-hit bomb in April 1941.

In the new Borough Council, William Duncan, a local builder, was one of the elected Mayors; and later Alderman H.T. Parkin piloted the procedures for the formation of the new London Borough of Bromley, of which he became Charter Mayor in 1965.

Mr G.W. Tookey, QC, made valuable contributions to our local history through his untiring research at the County Archives and subsequently passing on his findings to the Local library and, indeed, to many local history enthusiasts. For a number of years until his death in 1976 he was President of the Beckenham Branch of the Historical Association.

Beckenham has played a great part in the swimming world since the 1920s. Mr H.R. Austin, the Baths Superintendent for many years from about 1910, was himself a great swimmer and coached many others. He kept up his swimming until late in life, as did his contemporary Mr H. Morris, a schoolmaster at Beckenham County School for Boys; through his regular early-morning swims over several decades he was given a free pass by the Council. Mr Raymond Brown, a great worker in the 1920s among the young people of Christ Church, helped many enthusiasts at the Beckenham Baths. More recently Duncan Goodhew, a member of the Beckenham Swimming Club, gained a gold medal at the 1980 Olympics.

Some readers may remember the name of Sidney Box and Betty Box in the world of cinema. Sidney's father was a nurseryman at Kent House in the early 'twenties, and Sidney himself, as a boy, was a scorer for the Wesleyan Cricket Club.

The father of Robin Knox-Johnston, the round-the-world lone yachtsman, was Mayor of Beckenham in 1957. In the realm of entertainment, Sir Geraint Evans, the operatic singer, once lived in Beckenham, as did film-star Julie Andrews and popular singer Petula Clark, both of whom were educated in Beckenham during the 1950s. Bob Monkhouse's family lived in Bromley Road. Before he was educated at Dulwich College, in the 1940s, Bob attended the Sunday School at Beckenham Methodist Church.

And so one could go on. But in conclusion let it be said to those who would exclaim, 'What about so-and-so and so-and-so' – the answer may be revealed in a future publication!

Shortlands Waterworks, then (circa 1974) complete with beam engines (permission: M.V. Searle)

Shortlands Village

Shortlands is still The Village to old-established inhabitants, as it has always been, even since its building up as a suburb wedged between Beckenham and Bromley. We do not go to the shops – we go Down the Village. The view from under the railway bridge looking towards Valley School and the heights of Highland Road is remarkably little changed in its larger essentials compared with pictures taken fifty years ago, and there are still Victorian cottages with front gardens sitting between the shops, most of which are privately owned.

Such changes as have inevitably taken place have in general been lesser ones – losses of ordinary things or humble buildings of character, put to new uses so that they are the same and yet not the same.

Shortlands old water-works in Valley Road, built around 1867, looks almost exactly as it did when the second pumping-station was added following the sinking of a third well in 1917. But when one looks back into childhood something is realised to be missing: projecting from an arch above the east face of the old station were massive iron beam-arms which once drove the pumping machinery. I can just remember them in the operational days, slowly and rhythmically moving up and down to the muffled bonk-bonk of leisured movement. For many years they remained in place unused, but they were removed during recent restoration work; in 1983 one was mounted in the waterworks' garden for permanent display.

Two other interesting buildings of old Shortlands still exist without being easily recognised for what they once were. Almost facing the waterworks across the railway from the corner of Station Road and Martins Road was Shortlands Laundry, whose main building is intact except for the removal of its long skinny chimney. Children of the inter-wars period loved the laundry because it was still driven at least partially by steam. Low down on the main wall in Station Road can be seen a puzzling small square of filled-in brickwork, distinguishable as some sort of former window. In steam days it was filled not by glass but by a wooden hatch which was usually open during working hours. Even a small child could see through into a dark underworld of machinery and moving belts, only half visible in the all-pervading vapour of steam hanging over everything. The scent of clean white steam was as refreshing as that of the clean linen which was delivered back home after an investment of just a few pence for a shirt or a sheet. The building is now occupied by a clothing factory and a motor workshop.

Hidden up a narrow alleyway off The Village towards Queen's Mead is a tiny old brick building whose door is usually padlocked. It seems too small ever to have housed community activities; yet this was once All Saints Mission, whose old character as a chapel is better appreciated from the side through the enclosing fence. A crazy leaning iron chimney still pokes from the roof, probably once serving an old-fashioned stove. It seems a long time now since children gathered there for Sunday school, reading Bible verses round in a circle by turn, or scratching out sacred scenes in an old fasioned sand-tray. Yet it was still used as such until about eight years ago, when local people went there to sing unpretentious chapel hymns to the accompaniment of a piano.

Almost under the mission's side wall the little River Ravensbourne once trickled in a curve from Queen's Mead towards Shortlands station; shallow, full of pebbles, supporting the occasional tiddler for which small boys hopefully fished. The river is now invisible, imprisoned under a concrete culvert after leaving the Mead; but the line of this culverting still describes a curve here, showing that the water follows its old course under ground.

Another disused church hall-cum-chapel survived until about 1982 in Bromley Gardens, where two new houses near a railway footbridge mark its site. Attached to St Mary's church, it stood derelict for some years, progressively destroyed by children breaking in. It was saddening to see its handsome main window smashed again and again, and its remaining fittings flung broken into an alley. It was finally demolished only about two years ago. Between the two world wars St Mary's hall, like All Saints mission, was popular as a Sunday school, much patronised by small girls wearing straw best hats with flowers on their brims. During the week it served community purposes, and could be hired for large-scale birthday and other celebrations, easily catered for from a well equipped integral kitchen, and having an upright piano for community singing.

Older residents vividly remember watching a Nazi doodlebug throb over Shortlands during the 1939-45 war, cutting out its engine as it passed over Queen Anne Avenue, the signal meaning that its fall and explosion were imminent. It landed on St Mary's church, virtually demolishing it though leaving the tower and spire more or less intact. It is said that these were removed soon afterwards as dangerous structures. The writer as a small child post-war could thus boast of having jumped over St Mary's spire and back again; the secret was that the spire, its tapered top almost intact, was left lying in the derelict churchyard with the rest of the rubble, so that it could indeed be climbed on or jumped over from ground level.

Another amenity of the more recent past was the old fire station, yet already a generation exists which does not know that Shortlands once had it own brigade and engine, based at the corner of Martins Road. The disused station lasted well after the second World War, on a now empty site adjoining a small supermarket in Martins Road. This charming little station, no bigger than the average house, had a single arched stall for the engine. Long after this village brigade was merged into the bigger Beckenham or Bromley service, the building was named The Old Fire Station; I believe that it then served as a private house.

Queen's Mead before the mid-1950s was used much more for events than it is today. Until about 1953 funfairs regularly pitched on the railway side, with all the traditional amusements of roundabouts, chairoplanes and boat swings, a few driven by steam. They were the last of a long line of pleasure events, which in the previous generation had included a monster 'bun fight' party for all Shortlands children on the occasion of Edward VII's coronation in 1902, when hundreds of youngsters in their best smocks and buttoned black boots sat outdoors at trestle tables to celebrate in food and drink; yet the song from that day which old Shortlands people always recalled was peculiarly unchildlike:

We'll all be merry
Drinking whisky, wine and sherry,
On Coronation Day,
On Coronation Day.

For the 1937 coronation of George VI every child in Valley School was individually photographed and the prints sold to parents, presented in white folders printed with the Union Jack and, appropriately for a child's picture, drawings of the two little princesses. A mammoth firework display was mounted in the evening, using Martins Hill as a natural grandstand for viewing set-pieces mounted on the Hop Field below (this having once been the nearest hop garden to London). The finale was a large set-piece showing the new King and Queen in light.

The Ravensbourne in this part of Shortlands was a beautiful stream until less then twenty years ago. Not once but twice it has been harshened where it crosses the Mead: once by loss of the tall elm trees that shaded it, victims of Dutch elm disease; and secondly by necessary concrete canalisation following several damaging floods. We who lost property and furniture in the worst flood, in 1968, were only too relieved to see the flood prevention works completed; yet we still mourn the passing of the Ravensbourne's rural beauty.

Shortlands shops in general continue to look untownlike, successors of village stores of the near past. It seems but yesterday that a grocery shop in the main street was so cool and dark with high banks of crowded shelves, biscuits sold loose by the pound from ranks of square tin boxes with glass tops, and change given by means of a rattling overhead railway, on whose wires metal cannisters were catapulted from counter to cashier in a flash and shot back, the container being unscrewed to extract the money and receipt.

At the fish shop, whose floor was deep in sawdust, throughout the 1950s money was taken at a separate cubicle of a cash desk by a woman imprisoned there all day in her little cell while cash was passed to and fro through a small opening in the glass.

Even such small houses as those in Recreation Road were sometimes adapted as modest little businesses, notably between the two wars. At a miniature sweet-shop in a front parlour, children on their way to Valley

*The Personal Touch! A mobile greengrocery in urban Shortlands,
circa 1976 (permission: M.V. Searle)*

School in the 1930s stopped to buy such snacks as a farthing Golly Bar,
purchased with a coin whose value is now less than valueless; a Golly
Bar was a narrow and very thin flat stick of toffee.

In Bromley Gardens was the Binello grocery store, which in the 1950s
crammed enough stock for a small supermarket into one downstairs
room of an adapted house, served in the traditional way from behind a
counter. At one time several shops existed in this now residential road,
apart from the remaining sub-post office; it is still possible to observe
how two houses at the Ridley Road end were once shops, with their
larger windows; the grocery store and a one-time greengrocery shop.
There was also once a butchery in this Shortlands backwater.

I also recall at least two countrified smallholdings within the confines
of surburbia; a piggery under the high railway embankment in
Ravensbourne Avenue, acquired for housing some twenty years ago;
and a flower nursery at the foot of Bromley Road which gave way to
several blocks of flats about fifteen years ago. The nursery's holly hedge
was retained for enclosing the flats' communal open ground and some of
the frontages.

Many individualistic features of Shortlands have gone or have been
changed in the past three decades or less; yet enough remain to justify
keeping the old colloquial name of The Village. One need only stop and
buy vegetables from a mobile greengrocery that could belong to deepest
Kent, or patronise one of the two sub-post offices, or drop into the
village sweet-shop at school turning-out time to realise that. It is also
possible to see how history is made under our eyes, even in this modern
world: in Martins Road even the kerb-stones are now history; still
painted alternately red, white and blue for a 1977 Royal Jubilee street
party, they have never yet been changed back to colourless uniformity.

This is how Shortlands history had always been written: not by
national heroes but by ordinary people from ordinary homes who count
themselves villagers and keep a close community spirit.

Wartime Beckenham

Seven years before war broke out I joined the Metropolitan Special Constabulary at Penge: I was at this time (November 1932) one year under the legal minimum age. My first duty was one hour on the cross-roads outside Penge Police Station. I remember standing between the tram-lines and waving on the tram, much to the amusement of the driver.

As the War drew nearer, we had training in Air Raid Precautions and in how to use a gas-mask. At the beginning of September 1939 I decided that, although I was qualified as a chartered accountant, I would be more useful in full-time service with the Police.

On 3 September we heard the sirens a few minutes after Neville Chamberlain's announcement over the radio that war had been declared. On this occasion it was a false alarm, although the official explanation was that an unidentified 'plane had crossed the south coast. We had another warning a few days later at about three o'clock in the morning, and then came the period until the summer of 1940 known as the Phoney War. This was a deadly dull time. The winter of 1939-1940 was very severe, and on many nights when I was on duty it was a real pleasure to find the baker's shop in Thayers Farm Road. The wall was always very warm and comfortable to stand by.

At the time of Dunkirk I volunteered to work over the weekend on preparing ration-books. An interesting job was dealing with changes of address since the National Registration. Under the terms of the Official Secrets Act we were sworn to secrecy, as we found out who was living together without being married and who had been in prison at the time of registration.

Then the bombing started, at first at Biggin Hill and Croydon. I was looking out of my bedroom window one evening in August 1940 when I saw a squadron of 'planes flying in four flights of three in line astern. I thought that they were Spitfires, but then bombs fell from the 'planes onto Croydon Aerodrome.

A few nights later – 28 August – I was on duty and we had one or two alerts without the siren sounding. It was still quiet around midnight, so Sergeant Gay and I decided to go home. He accompanied me to Clock House Station, the limit of Penge Manor. He was just about to go when I saw the searchlights looking for a 'plane coming from the south. We waited for a short time and then beat a hasty retreat to the brick shelter outside the station in Clock House Road, and then back to the station as bombs had been dropped. We then went to the Elmers End Cemetery and Sewage Farm to look for the bombs, as the people from the bus garage on the opposite side of Elmers End Road had told us that they were sure they had come down in the area as they had heard gravel falling on the roof. After about half an hour someone asked, 'What are you looking for?' 'The bombs', I replied, to which he said, 'They are not here, they are at the corner of Hampden Avenue and Cromwell Road'. This was too near my own home for comfort.

He was right: there had been two armour-piercing bombs. The first was between St. James's Avenue, Cromwell Road and Foster Road. Very little blast damage had been done, but huge chunks of clay had been blown to a great height and had fallen through the roof of one of the houses. In fact a friend of my brother's was awakened by the vibration as the bomb went off, and as he sat up in bed a very large lump of clay came through the roof and bedroom ceiling, and landed on his pillow.

The other bomb fell at the corner of Clock House Road and Hampden Road, just where I would have been if I had gone home instead of waiting to see what developed at Clock House Station. I then felt that I would survive the War. This bomb had demolished two houses. A child asleep under the stairs in a third house was right on the edge of the crater, but was protected by the mattress. Some casualties were blown up into the trees at the bottom of the garden. Furniture was blown over the houses opposite on to the railway line.

My brother, a member of the Auxiliary Fire Service, found himself under the bed, again from the vibration of the explosion. The Anderson shelter in our family's garden had just been concreted and there was some doubt as to whether it had dried out, but my mother had decided to sleep out there in spite of the fact that there had been no official warning of raids that night. The next she knew was a voice calling, 'Are you all right in there, Mrs. Tuffrey?' 'Of course I'm all right', she replied. 'It's raining, isn't it?' It was, but not raindrops – bricks, telephone directories and even pound notes were falling from a great height.

The first big raid on London was on 7 September 1940, followed by the start of the night bombing. Lawrie Park Road was hit. A further big raid was on 15 September. The first 'plane that night dropped bombs on the Elmers End Cemetery, and I was looking for unexploded bombs when the really big raid came. It was a frightening sight to see the masses of bombers and fighters coming into London from the east. A large number of bombs were dropped on the railway line at Kent House, from Kings Hall Road up to the Penge Tunnel, which was pierced. From then on we had an incident every day up to Christmas Eve.

Just before the blitz really started we had a lecture on Air Raid Precautions in the Odeon Cinema at Elmers End. We sang *God Save The King* and then an ex-Royal Navy seaman, who had been a leader of the Invergordon Mutiny in the Fleet against the ten per cent pay cut in 1931, told us what to expect in an air raid. His advice was very different from the official instruction book. Amongst other advice he gave was,

'If the siren goes, go to sleep again unless you hear gunfire; don't worry about sealing up cracks round the window against gas – if gas is used you will not have any windows; the fire-bombs can be put out easily, but not if you sit in shelters and do not see where they fall.' All good advice. 'If you see either a straight smoke line or a smoke circle in the sky, watch out, for the bombers will use that as a signal where to bomb.' When we came out of the cinema there was the line in the sky, and the bombs began to fall.

One very nasty incident was when a full canister of 1,320 incendiaries fell on a house in Cottingham Road, right through the stairs. The warden was there, but he was completely and utterly unable to help in any way due to the intense heat, and his wife and child were under the stairs.

Another night a bomb demolished houses in Kings Hall Road, and the residents were in a Morrison shelter. I was surprised how weak their voices seemed when they called for help.

On another occasion I was visiting my grandmother at 71 Kings Hall Road when the siren sounded. On my way back to the station the bombs began to fall and I was able to report their effect: no damage except to a partly-built private air raid shelter where the walls had been blown about six inches out of true. The remaining bombs were all on a sports ground between New Beckenham and Lower Sydenham.

This was the last of the bad night raids on 6 May 1941. My father had his hair cut by a lady from Kendall Road. It was her daughter's twenty-first birthday party and the whole night was spent in the air raid shelter. The all-clear did not sound at daybreak, although there had been no activity for more than an hour. The party decided to leave the shelter, with the exception of the 21-year-old daughter, who would not leave before the all-clear. A bomb fell on the house, and everyone was killed except the girl in the shelter. Immediately afterwards the all-clear sounded.

The next period of activity was the invasion of Normandy, followed by the flying bombs. We had a flying bomb which fell between Hampden Road, Clock House Road and Queens Road. It took out all our windows and removed most of the roof. This was at mid-day on a Friday. On Saturday morning the first-aid building repair squad arrived and set to work with tarred paper to make the houses wind- and water-tight. On Saturday night another flying bomb fell almost in the same place. All the tarred paper was blown off, plus the few remaining tiles. The repair squad arrived in their buses, but they never set to work with the same will to protect our property.

Heavy casualties resulted from the destruction of Elmers End Bus Garage in Elmers End Road, Birkbeck, by a flying bomb. This tragedy, on 18 July 1944, was one of the worst single incidents of the War suffered by the London Passenger Transport Board. I was the first police officer on the scene.

Another very bad incident was the bomb that fell in Beckenham Road between Sidney Road and Churchfields Road. My father had been a customer of Hancock's Fish Shop for twenty-five years, and just half an hour earlier he had been in the shop buying fish.

As the flying bomb (V1) attack died down the Rocket (V2) attack began. Seven of these weapons fell on Beckenham, but very few people were killed as they fell mainly on open spaces, such as the sports grounds owned by various banks at New Beckenham.

I left Beckenham on 1 January 1948, when I married, and I have very recently (1983) retired from Hope, Agar and Company, Accountants, after more than fifty years – the War years excepted – with one firm. In that time I rose from Office Boy to second Senior Partner out of twelve.

The Chinese Garage

One of several curious facts about the landmark known as 'the Chinese Garage' is that it is not really Chinese. More correctly it ought to be known as the Japanese Garage (if not given its proper commercial name of Park Langley Garage); but to everybody who has known it during the past half century or so it will always be simply the Chinese Garage.

With its delicate pagoda roofs and oriental decorations, it is, for a stranger, as unexpected a sight in the midst of suburbia as a giraffe in Oxford Circus. Yet the Japanese theme of the garage and its gardens is said to have been devised to blend in with the existing character of the district; an unlikely theory at first sight, for nothing could be less oriental than the mixture of remaining countryside with new suburban roads which comprised the Beckenham of 1928.

This explanation becomes clearer, however, when it is remembered how the owner of Langley spent some considerable time in Japan and, like other rich travellers and landowners of his generation, determined to bring something of its graceful decorative styles and garden layouts back to his home estate. Accordingly the grounds of Langley Court were laid out with a wealth of new Japanese plants and shrubs, to simulate the gardens of the east, which apparently thrived in the reasonably mild climate of West Kent.

In turn this Japanese influence spread into the immediately surrounding area as it changed over from its age-old country life into a generally fairly moneyed new suburb-land of big houses, whose builders could afford to add little extra conceits for decoration's sake. Japanese style ornamentation thus appeared in imitation of the Langley Court work, notably in the lamp-posts and letter-boxes of Wickham Way and other nearby roads.

Carrying the same theme on again, and more prominently into the notice of the general public, a new garage, serving a community well able to afford cars when they were far from universal, was also built to complement the mixture of an English suburb with foreign overtones. Park Langley Garage was erected by Henry Fox Taylor for his son in 1928, just as Beckenham and Park Langley were being swallowed by the inexorable march of the builders. The Taylor family building firm was indeed responsible for much of the Park Langley estate itself. The site was formerly occupied by Stone Farm, which is commemorated by Stone Park Avenue, built soon afterwards.

Initially Park Langley Garage served only as a filling station, but six years later in 1934 it was extended to include workshops at the rear for repair and maintenance of cars, as they appeared in gradually increasing numbers on the road.

The Chinese Garage today (permission: M.V. Searle)

*Above: The workshops at the Chinese Garage, circa 1930
(permission both pictures: M.V. Searle)*

Below: The first works outing from the Chinese Garage, 1933

The proprietors quickly realised that the existing railway could be tapped to provide additional custom, rather than regarded as a stealer of trade from the roads. They started their own bus, running from the garage to Beckenham Junction station, complete with a liveried driver, as a service to clients who could drive to Park Langley, leave their cars to be serviced during the day, catch their trains by courtesy of the private bus, and collect the cars again in due course. The non-motoring public could also use this bus service to save themselves a mile walk to the station, for the cheap fare of just one old penny.

Here was service with style as well as with a smile. Smartness of dress and appearance were required of even a garage employee in the days when casual dress at work was almost unthinkable. The breakdown truck was nothing less than a Rolls, whose driver went on the job in a smart uniform instead of working overalls. Petrol pump attendants were again turned out in proper uniforms for the benefit of clients, with peaked caps on their short-cropped heads, well drilled in the maxim that the customer was always right.

Equipment kept pace with the fast moving times of the 1930s, and the garage acquired by the early Thirties one of the first hydraulic vehicle hoists.

During the 1939-45 war the garage, like other enterprises having suitable workshop accommodation, undertook its share of war work. Aircraft and gun parts were made here towards the war effort, greatly helped by the garage having its own generating equipment, making it independent of erratic normal supplies.

Innovations were still being made into the 1960s, when a filling station, lubrication bays and showroom were opened on the other side of Stone Park Avenue. From the beginning it had been associated with the Austin Motor Company, which in time joined forces with Morris as the British Motor Corporation, and finally became a part of British Leyland.

Today the so-called Chinese Garage is still as unexpected as that giraffe in the centre of London, though to the drivers of passing buses it is as common a destination request as the High Street, almost always under its colloquial name. However familiar, it intrigues the eye afresh at every visit, with its little oriental pagoda sitting on top of its elegantly shaped eastern roofs, all curves and dips. Around its well kept courtyard are a series of big white stone lanterns, likewise in Japanese vein, lending their own air of fantasy to what would normally be the most mundane of services.

"The Scooter Run"
The Story of a Beckenham Bus Route

In many respects Beckenham was still a country town when, at the turn of the century, the sight and sound of motor vehicles brought the first murmurings of change. A road transport change which, within a mere couple of decades, would virtually sweep away the horse-drawn vehicle.

It was not long before this advancing transport revolution was manifested in Beckenham by the appearance of the town's first motor-buses, which commenced to thread their way through the High Street in 1914. The clattering intruders were single deck buses, and for the greater part of the past 70 years they and their generations of successors have been a familiar feature of the local street scene. Certainly, the little buses have long been identified by the people whose locality they serve with the number of the route which they follow. For more than 50 years the buses on this route have had bestowed upon them an obvious yet subtle identity; something which somehow sets them apart from their identical contemporaries plying bus routes all over London and the suburbs. These buses are, in the parlance of those who use them and know them best, just – 'the 227s'.

Single-deck AEC B-type bus on the original 109 route at Beckenham Church in London General Omnibus Company Livery, 1925 (permission: H.R. Copeland)

A petrol-electric Tilling Stevens bus on route 109 at Penge, 1932
(permission: Sheaf Publishing)

It was on 1 June 1914 that the London General Omnibus Company introduced the new route between Thicket Road, Penge and the 'White Hart' in Bromley. At the outset the new bus service was numbered 112 and was worked by three 20 seat vehicles. They were in fact a development of the 'B' type London General omnibus, the first really successful and reliable London motor-bus and a vehicle which was destined to leave its mark on history in more than just the transport sense. During World War One hundreds of these buses served in France, many of them driven by their own London bus drivers. It is recorded that during the furious and bloody battles of the autumn of 1914 the driver of one of the London 'B' types personally captured 12 Germans and drove them into captivity on the top deck of his bus. 'Old Bill' was the nickname that the Tommies gave to the familiar 'B' type which trundled so many of them to and tragically, not so many from, the trenches. Thereafter, the 'B' type would forever be known as 'Old Bill'.

In 1914, therefore, it was not surprising when less than three months after the first motor-buses chugged through the streets of Beckenham – they suddenly disappeared. Within two weeks of the outbreak of war on 4 August the three new Beckenham buses were requisitioned by the War Office and sent to France where they served as military ambulances. They never returned to the peaceful roads of Beckenham. No replacements were forthcoming and for the next two years Beckenham's first brief encounter with the motor-bus languished.

By 1916 Woolwich Arsenal was fully stretched producing the munitions of war and drawing labour from a wide area. Although

The bus for which the term 'Scooter' was first coined: an LT-type AEC Regal at Penge shortly before withdrawal, 1952 (permission: Sheaf Publishing)

somewhat distant from the Arsenal, Beckenham and Penge could supply some of the hands that were so desparately needed and so, in August 1916, motor-buses reappeared on the former Beckenham bus route. This time six second-hand 'Old Bill' buses were converted from double to single deck and, on a route which was then re-numbered 109, commenced to rumble their way between Penge and Woolwich by way of Beckenham, Bromley, Chislehurst and Eltham. One of the drawbacks of these makeshift vehicles was that they only provided 16 seats.

Double deck buses, which would have provided more than twice that number of seats, could not be used because of the low railway bridges in Beckenham Road and at Shortlands. Another obstacle was the narrow arch which spanned the main road at the top of Summer Hill near Chislehurst. This arch had been erected in the 1860s by George Wythes, a local landowner who had his own reasons for wanting to restrict the flow of traffic over his land. Ostensibly the massive brick arch which he built was supposed to be a water-tower although, because of the availability of a mains supply, it is doubtful whether George Wythes's creation ever supplied water to anybody. However, it did provide an 'eye of a needle' road restriction only of sufficient width to allow the passage of one vehicle; it was certainly not high enough to accommodate a double deck bus – even if the bus did have an open top!

With the Armistice in 1918 and the end of the war the demands on Woolwich Arsenal subsided from a torrent to a trickle, with the result

Not quite what it seems . . . this Victorian horse-bus came out of retirement for the Charter Celebrations, 1935. Does it still survive somewhere today? (permission: H.R. Copeland)

that, in February 1919, the 109 bus service was again withdrawn. The strength of the public outcry which ensued demonstrated how much the buses had proved their worth and, seven months later, these protests brought back the 109s on a re-opened route between Penge and Bromley North.

For the next 19 years the 109 route was extended and squeezed, sometimes with bewildering frequency, as the bus company 'tested the market'. During this period the terminal points of the route fluctuated between extremities which reached Forest Hill at one end and Welling at the other. Eventually, in 1925, the 'Crooked Billet' in Penge was settled upon as the inner terminus of the route.

In 1926 the outer extremity was extended from Chislehurst to Eltham, where it remained until 1933. In that year the little buses went even further afield and for the next five years they wended their long way between Penge and Welling. Intensive housing development enveloped vast areas of metropolitan North Kent during the 1930s, with the result that bus passengers at the Welling end of the route out-stripped the resources of the hard-worked single deckers. Consequently, in 1938, the 'Welling extension' was handed over to double decked buses which worked it as a separate route and, ever since, the Beckenham single

112, 109, 227 — BUSES —

PRINCIPAL CHANGES IN ROUTE SINCE 1914

*Hansom cabs at Beckenham Junction Station, still plying for hire in 1925!
(permission: H.R. Copeland)*

deckers have rested and turned round at the 'Gordon Arms', Chislehurst.

In 1934 the route was re-numbered 227. This was a direct consequence of a rationalisation exercise carried out by the new public transport undertaking which had gone into business in 1933. In that year the independent and municipal public transport operators, who had hitherto run the majority of the capital's bus, tram, trolleybus and underground railway services, were amalgamated by Act of Parliament to become the London Passenger Transport Board. With the formation of the LPTB Londoners saw the last of the old independent bus companies which, on 1 July 1933, vanished overnight when red painted buses bearing the legend 'London Transport' took to the road. They are, of course, still there.

The outbreak of hostilities on 3 September 1939 did not, as in 1914, rob the route of its buses, and the 227s continued to shuttle between Penge and Chislehurst. The appearance of the buses took on a distinctive wartime aspect with heavily hooded headlights and, to begin with, practically no light at all inside the bus. The side windows were covered with glued-on gauze (to minimise the glass splintering effects of bomb blast) which meant that passengers could only see where they were by peering through small diamond shaped apertures which were left uncovered by the obscuring gauze. After dark dim, blue internal lights barely enabled the bus conductor to see to issue tickets, and reading on a wartime bus at night was out of the question. Passengers in front seats were, however, afforded a clear view ahead. They were presumably reassured about the danger from flying glass by a notice

. . . and their successor, the ubiquitous Austin motor taxi of the 1930's, again at Beckenham Junction (permission: H.R. Copeland)

stuck on the front windows of the bus. It informed, somewhat hopefully, that 'This window is made of toughened glass'.

At that time the 227s were six-wheeled (3 axled) 'LT' type buses which had been introduced on the route in 1934. These 35 seaters gave sterling service throughout the Second World War – and indeed for a long time before and after. The last 'LT' scootered its way through Beckenham in 1952, the buses having by then monopolised the 227 route for 18 years. Busmen at Elmers End Garage, which was the home of the 227s from 1938 until 1952, had dubbed the fast and efficient LT's as 'scooters' and the route became known to busmen as 'The Scooter Run'.

In late 1952 the LT's vanished from route 227 with the introduction of new underfloor engine vehicles known as the 'RF' type, operated from Bromley Garage rather than Elmers End. The RF's gave good service for just as long as their worthy predecessors, being replaced in January 1971 by a one-man operated single-decker – the SMS, about which the less said the better. Suffice to say that the SMS type lasted only six years on the 227 route. Its departure, unmourned by passenger and busman alike, was followed in 1977 by the Leyland National 'LS' type, which still operates the route in 1984 and seems set to pound 'The Scooter Run' into the 1990s.

Since 1951 the 'Penge – Crooked Billet' destination blind of the 227s has heralded the route's inner terminus with lessening frequency. From that year some 227 journeys were extended from the 'Billet' to the central bus terminal at Crystal Palace, an improvement of great benefit to passengers in Beckenham and Penge who were then able to travel to the major bus interchange by way of a single bus journey.

At the 'country' end of the route the terminus remains, as it has since 1938, at the 'Gordon Arms', Chislehurst, the 227s having by then crossed Chislehurst Common which still lends to that part of the journey a certain rural aspect. Back in the 1930s single deck London Transport buses were seldom seen on in-town bus routes, although they were a familiar enough sight in the surburban and green belt environs of the city. In those days London Transport red single deckers were often referred to as 'country buses' and the 227s were no exception. Now of course London Transport's single deckers roam all over the London bus network; they are just as likely to be seen shuffling through the traffic jams of Central London as they may be seen ambling along the byways of London's outer periphery. Even though the present day 227 route is entirely suburban, its character in some peculiar way manages to retain the hint of a country bus. The 227 is the sort of bus that, in imagination and on a bright summer's day, one might take to flee the dusty streets of town. There is about the 'scooters', still, a sort of arcadian charm; something special to those quite ordinary London buses as they wend their way through Beckenham to Bromley – and beyond.

Further information and photographs relating to Route 227 and other local bus services can be found in *Bus Crew*, edited by J.S. Wagstaff and published by Sheaf Publishing, 35 Mooroaks Road, Sheffield, S10 1BX, 1979 (price £2.50).

Last Days of the Elmers End to Sanderstead Branch

On Friday, 13 May 1983, a chapter of local transport history came to an end, with the permanent closure of the branch railway from Elmers End southwards to Selsdon and Sanderstead.

This was one of the few new closures to be made since the universal wielding of Beeching's Axe over the railways of Britain in the 1960s.

Between about 1960 and 1970, taking obituary journeys over railways which were about to be shut down was much practised among enthusiasts who, if possible, aimed at being there to travel on the last train of the last operational day. But in 1983 such a trip was an isolated experience, not to be easily repeated. The writer was among those who, in the last few days of this branch of Southern Region, joined the camera-slung throng for a final return journey, down to Sanderstead and back. Some of the intermediate stations already wore a depressed air, half deserted even before the official closure date; their mournfulness was disturbed but not dispelled by any briefly stopping train, only to descend more heavily than ever once it had pulled away.

According to BR's own data, the main part of this short line, the section between the junction at Woodside and Selsdon, was opened on 10 August 1885, under a joint London Brighton and South Coast Railway and South Eastern Railway arrangement.

Elmers End station itself was far removed from the suburban stopping point of today, surrounded by miles of open agricultural countryside, with Penge and Beckenham as its nearest villages, both in their infancy of residential growth. A healthy freight business thus grew up, in addition to passenger traffic, transporting farm produce and milk to London.

Even in those early days, public brickbats were regularly lobbed at the railway by passengers, notably those concerning cleanliness of the carriages. The compulsive railway grumbler could never accept that dirty carriages usually resulted from litter-lout passengers rather than the railway company. It was, however, believed that one particular group of complainers through the national press were passengers who harboured some special grudge against this company, having recently been prosecuted for 'cheating the railway', presumably through fare evasion; adverse publicity designed to undermine the company was their method of getting their own back.

Nor were graffitists unknown, for as far back as 1857, before the opening of the Selsdon branch, staff rules were laid down – and duly followed when this line was built – whereby each stationmaster was duty bound to inspect his platform lavatories for 'unseemly writings or sketchings'.

Evidence of these early days lingered on at Elmers End decades after the South Eastern Railway ceased independently to exist, in an historic

Above: Platford signalbox at Sanderstead, shortly before final closure, 1983 (permission: M.V. Searle)

Below: A deserted platform at Bingham Road a few days before the end, May 1983 (permission: M.V. Searle)

station seat still labelled 'SER' for South Eastern Railway. It was believed to be an original item of station furniture dating from the building of Elmers End in 1864; the purpose of Elmers End then was mainly to provide a railhead for direct services to London over the then Croydon and London Branch of the SER, as far as Addiscombe Road.

By the late nineteenth century suburbia first began encircling this rural branch, notably near Coombe Road and Selsdon Road stations. By 1906, Wainwright steam railmotors were in use, running up to the Woodside junction. To accommodate them, new wooden halts were opened in 1906 serving Bingham Road and the now long-lost Spencer Road (between Selsdon Road and Coombe Lane, as Coombe Road was then known). Spencer Road lacked even an approach road, served only by footpaths.

Build a railway, and houses would follow, spawning customers, reasoned the average company, but in this case the formula did not work.

A foretaste of things to come occurred between the two world wars, when the Selsdon and Sanderstead line was closed for a long period, during which it earned its local nickname of The Ghost Line, through the handful of freight trains still occasionally disturbing the silence.

The Great War was a golden excuse for ending the railmotor service from 1915, when the smaller halts closed, though the line remained open for one further year. The section between Woodside and the then Selsdon Road stations was closed from 1 January 1917 and not reopened until 30 September 1935, a period of eighteen years. After the war the line continued closed to normal services, but again saw rare special trains, notably hop pickers' trains cashing in on the then huge scale Kentish hop season, when all the bines were picked by hand, by armies of East Enders taken down by train for a working holiday; the only one they ever knew. Hop specials brought every railway in Kent a handsome profit.

Re-laying of the badly worn track was begun in 1927, raising false hopes, yet still no regular trains appeared. When at last the line did open again, in 1935, it was not to steam; electrification, already extended through most of what was then the Southern Railway, was the new order of the day.

The new electric service gave half hourly trains – three in the rush hours – some running straight on to London instead of interchanging at Woodside. Hopeful of increasing revenue from the mushrooming miles of suburbia between Croydon and Beckenham, the company rebuilt Bingham Road Halt as a full station, but on the debit side the little used Spencer Road Halt was abandoned. Coombe Lane became Coombe Road, and Selsdon Road was renamed as Selsdon; which did nothing to lessen the fact that Selsdon proper was still two miles away from its station. In general, the public failed to support the line, an unusual phenomenon in mushrooming suburbia.

Beeching's Axe almost fell as early as around 1963, as usage went on declining, when the branch was earmarked for abandonment despite being so near London. Only a long and vociferous protest campaign saved it for another two decades of service to the community, which celebrated its reprieve by using the trains less and less, as cars became universal from the early Sixties onwards.

It became increasingly apparent that BR's ultimate aim must be closure. An air of running down descended, heavily emphasised by the mornings- and evenings-only nature of the reduced latter-day timetables. There was virtually no call for trains at other hours of the day. Scarcely anyone but commuters bothered with the line; trade became almost exclusively tied up with work in London, and with children going to school.

At about the same period part of Elmers End station was badly damaged by fire, but this was rebuilt to today's more utility pattern and, of course, remains busily in use to serve two out of its original three lines, those to Addiscombe and to Hayes.

Finally closure was announced for 13 May 1983. The obsequies of the last day were in the tradition of railway closures of the Sixties. Former and present regular passengers were almost crowded out of the jam packed carriages by hoardes of railway enthusiasts, who thronged the normally almost empty compartments of electric multiple unit number 5720 on its final round trip down towards Woodside where the Sanderstead line branched off into what is now railwayless territory. They passed through antiquated stations which, like the line itself, prematurely wore an air of emptiness despite the photographers on their normally deserted platforms.

Over two hundred jostled onto the last train; as BR rightly said, had the trains been used normally as they were in their last six weeks of existence, closure would not have happened.

As the final train drew in to Elmers End, a farewell toast of champagne was handed to the driver, guard and stationmaster; no celebration toast, but rather a funereal party gesture. It did not go unnoticed that the day was Friday the Thirteenth.

Information and photographs relating to other local railways, past and present, will be found in two books by Muriel Searle. These are:

Down the Line to Dover, published by Baton Press Limited, 44 Holden Park Road, Southborough, Tunbridge Wells, Kent, 1983 (price £8.95).

Lost Lines, published by New Cavendish Books, 23 Craven Hill, London, W.2., 1982 (price £9.95 hardback, £3.95 paperback).

Sport in Beckenham

For more than one hundred years there have been two centres for major sporting events in the area – Crystal Palace and the Beckenham Cricket Club in Foxgrove Road.

At Crystal Palace, where in the 1860s the great tightrope walker, Blondin, once cooked an omelette on a wire stretched the length of the central transept, tens of thousands of spectators came to watch the FA Cup Final before the First World War. The Cup Final subsequently moved to Wembley but, with the opening of the National Sports Centre at Crystal Palace in the 1960s, the Palace once again became a magnet for the leading national and international athletes, with world records on the track coming at times as regularly as rate-demands.

When the Sports Centre was first opened, interest in athletics tended to follow a four-year cycle of popular interest, rising before the Olympic Games and falling away sharply immediately afterwards. But with the development of the European Games and the Commonwealth Games, Crystal Palace has provided a steadier flow of top-level athletic competition year after year.

Inside Crystal Palace Sports Hall, the Beckenham swimmers have also continued to hold their own. The Beckenham Men's Swimming Club was founded in 1879 and the Ladies' Swimming Club in 1921. For more than three decades after the Second World War, the Beckenham Swimming Club and in particular the Beckenham Ladies have been in the top flight of national competition. Margaret Wellington is the first of a distinguished string of local Olympic competitors: Linda Ludgrove, Margaret Kelly, Chris Walkenden and Duncan Goodhew have all captured titles and medals. In 1984 13-year-old Club member Zara Long took part in the Olympics as the country's youngest-ever swimming entrant. Historians of the future may point to the superb facilities at Crystal Palace as one reason for the Beckenham swimmers' spectacular success. In fact, the Olympic pool is used only for long-course squad training; most of the other club training takes place in local pools.

In 1866, thirteen years before the formation of the first Beckenham Swimming Club, the Beckenham Cricket Club had started. The first recorded game took place on 19 May of that year against Meriden Single Members, with ten men playing on each side. In those days there was no declaration rule in force, and a side continued batting regardless of the state of the game. Thus in 1880 Upper Tooting scored 485 runs in a single day but Beckenham did not bat, while in 1885 Beckenham scored 402 and Upper Tooting never got to the wicket.

Some of the best players in the country played against the Club. On 2 June 1894 the Club played against Hampstead Cricket Club side, which included A.E. Stoddart and F.R. Spofforth ('The Demon'). Stoddart made 148 of Hampstead's 269 runs, and Stoddard and Spofforth then bowled out Beckenham for thirteen and twenty-one, ten of which were byes. Spofforth took twelve wickets for eleven runs, and Stoddart eight wickets for twelve runs.

In 1899 W.G. Grace himself made 81 for Crystal Palace at Foxgrove Road, and 130 the following year. During World War One the Club closed down, though many members attended the funeral at Elmers End Cemetery of Dr W.G. Grace. Soon after the end of the 1914-18 War the Beckenham Cricket Club could field a team in which every member in the side had played for a county. After the Second World War perhaps the outstanding player to turn out for the Club team was Derek Underwood, who took seven for twenty-eight for the Club against Cyphers when he was just seventeen. A year earlier he had taken 101 wickets for Kent in a remarkable first season.

For thirty years since 1954, the Beckenham Hockey Club, which was founded in 1900, has ranked among the best in the country. Under the leadership of John Brazil, W. vans Agnew, A.G. Page, R.Y. Fison and R. Sutton, the Club has produced more than a score of international players and more than one hundred county caps.

But perhaps Foxgrove Road is best known for the international tennis tournament which began in 1886. The first champion was Henry Chipp, who went on to become a well-known Wimbledon umpire. 'The Field' described the final with E.J. Avlry, a Club committee member, as 'terribly tedious' as both players stayed at the back of the court and played with extreme caution. The tournament lost £1 10s 9d and the Secretary was told that the loss 'must not occur again'.

In fact the loss did not occur again and the leading players of the 1890s and 1900s did come back – the Renshaws, the Dochertys, Norman Brooks, A.W. Gore, A.F. Wilding and H. Roper-Barratt. All won titles at Beckenham before going on a few weeks later to win at Wimbledon. Bunny Austin won the Men's Championship in 1930 and again in 1934.

But between the Wars the Women's Championship produced an even more illustrious roll of winners than the Men's. Helen Wills, Dorothy Ryan and Alice Marble all won the trophy, while the final in 1920 between Elizabeth Ryan and Mrs. Lambert Chambers was said by some connoisseurs to be the greatest game of women's tennis ever seen.

After World War Two, Beckenham quickly re-established itself as the major stepping-stone on the way to Wimbledon. Frank Sedgman, Gardner Mulloy, Tony Travert, John Newcombe, Rod Laver, Jimmy Connors and Roscoe Tanner provided great tennis in a tournament which provides just enough incentive to bring out the best in players without the inhibiting tensions that sometimes afflict even the best players at Wimbledon or the other top tournaments. Some experts say that the year that Roscoe Tanner lost to Bjorn Borg in a classic final at Wimbledon, the Beckenham final between Roscoe Tanner and Jimmy Connors was even better.

Apart from producing superb tennis, Beckenham has also played its part in bringing innovation to a rapidly changing tennis scene. Laurie McCallum, who ran the tournament for so many years, played a major role in speeding the change to open tennis, and Beckenham itself staged the first open tournament played on grass. The Beckenham tennis tournament was the first to welcome competitors from the Soviet Union, and thanks to Rothmans it staged in 1961 the first sponsored tournament in this country.

Beckenham Tennis Week remains the central show-piece in a notable sporting calendar in a notable sporting area.

Extracts from West Kent Poll Books, 1847

Before the 1872 Ballot Act, which introduced to this country the secret ballot for political elections, the inquisitive could glean how local householders voted by a glance at the Poll Book. The letters at the head of each right-hand column represent the initials of the various candidates (the FAH were Messrs. Filmer, Austen and Hodges).

BROMLEY DISTRICT.

Beckenham. | F A H

Adams, John Dunkin, Elmer Lodge, Beckenham
Adams, Edward Richards, Elmer Lodge, Beckenham
Adams, Edward Richards, jun., 2, Lincoln's Inn, Old-square
Blake, John, Croydon, Surrey
Brandrum, Andrew, Rectory House, Beckenham
Cator, John, Beckenham-place
Cator, Albemarle, Woodbastwick, Norfolk
Cator, William, Limerick, Ireland
Cator, Peter
Chesterman, Horatio, Beckenham
Desborough, Henry, The Village, Beckenham
Foster, Richard Stewart, Langley-Lodge, Lewisham
Fowden, Reginald, Beckenham
Fuller, William, The Village, Beckenham
Fuller, Abraham, 11, Devonshire-street, Kennington
Gibbons, William, The Village, Beckenham —Dead
Gibbons, William, Fox Grove Farm
Goodman, Thomas, Dulwich
Goddard, John, Clock House, Beckenham
Goodhart, Emanuel, Langley Park, Beckenham
Goodhart, Charles Emanuel, Langley Park, Beckenham
Hardwick, Benjamin, 12, Montpelier-row, Blackheath
Hankey, George, Beckenham
Harding, James, near Penge Common, Beckenham
Hoare, Henry Meyrick, 37, Fleet-street
Hoare, Charles, 37, Fleet-street
Hoare, Peter Richard, Kelsey Park, Beckenham
Hollifield, Thos., Elmer's-end, Beckenham
Holland, Lancelot, Langley Farm, Beckenham
Jenner, Herbert, Kelsey Cottage, Beckenham
Joyce, John, High-street, Bromley
Latter, Robinson, Bromley
Latter, Henry, 5, Adelphi-terrace, Strand
Lawford, Edwd., Eden Park, Beckenham
Leach, Thomas, Beckenham
Levens, William, The Village, Beckenham
Loyd, Samuel Jones, Wickham Park, Addington
Miller, Wm. Grant, High-street, Marylebone
Miller, James, Guildford-place, Kennington, and 47, Eastcheap, London
Marshall, John, Eden Lodge, Beckenham
Mathew, Michael, Coper's Cope Farm, Beckenham

Beckenham. | F A H

Mathew, Michael, jun., Kent House Farm, Beckenham
Nix, John, Rock-hills, Beckenham
Overton, Henry, Surrey-street, Croydon
Overy, George, Beckenham
Ovenden, William, Beckenham
Paget, Peter, Elmer's-end, Beckenham
Peters, Wm., Beckenham-pl., Beckenham
Pullen, John, Penge-lane, near Sydenham
Russell, Robert, Sanderstead, near Croydon
Russell, Edward, Croydon
Russell, Thomas, Croydon
Russell, William, Croydon
Russell, John, Coulsdon, near Croydon
Russell, John, Norwood, Croydon
Russell, James, Arlglass, Down, Ireland
Russell, Robert, Coulsdon, Surrey
Russell, James, Arlglass, Down, Ireland
Russell, John, Norwood
Russell, John, Northend, Croydon
Rushton, Thomas, Beckenham
Scott, James, Clay-hill, Beckenham
Sidney, John Apsley, 53, Beaumont-street, London
Talman, James John, 2, Fir Grove-place, Brixton
Talman, Francis Henry, Beckenham
Tawke, Christian, Croydon
Titcomb, John, The Village, Beckenham
Turner, James, Elmer's End, Beckenham
Wathen, Hulbert, Beckenham
Wilson, Samuel, Village-place, Beckenham
Wilson, Cornelius Lee, ditto
Whitmore, William, near the Village, Beckenham
White, John, New Farm
Wright, William, 129, Grove-street, Camden Town, London
Wright, William, 2, Pitt's-place, Parson's-green, Fulham

Bromley.

Ashford, John, High-street, St. Paul, Deptford
Appleton, Thomas, Plaistow-lane
Ayling, Thomas, Bromley
Alexander, William, Bromley
Addis, Richard, Bromley
Boyd, Robert, esq., Plaistow Lodge, Bromley
Burton, Robert Barber, High-st., Bromley
Barnes, Thomas, 6, Clark's-place, Islington
Barrett, Richard, Bromley
Baxter, William, Bromley
Bilke, Henry, Stamford-street
Bilke, John, Stamford-street
Barber, Joseph, Clapham Rise

An Association of Ideas

John Wagstaff traces the beginnings of the Beckenham & Bromley Branch

Although there was an interval of more than forty years between the formation of the Historical Association in 1906 and that of the Beckenham branch in 1947, the latter can claim a spiritual link with the origins of the parent body in that one of our local members is the daughter of an Historical Association 'founding father', Professor T.F. Tout. Dr Margaret Sharp, who now lives in Sydenham, recalls accompanying her father to some of the very first meetings of the Association.

Over the years since 1906 the number of branches has steadily grown, so that there are now more than eighty in the British Isles and a further smattering as far afield as Australia, southern Africa and Canada. Membership stands at about ten thousand, and every Easter representatives of branches gather for a lively Annual Conference at one or other of our University towns.

Back in 1947, a resident of Park Road was to the Beckenham branch what Professor Tout had been to the Association. In the words of the late Mr Geoffrey Tookey, writing for the 1972 Silver Jubilee Edition of the Beckenham Historian as Branch president, 'With her progressive and outward-looking views, Miss Elizabeth Gundrey perceived the need for an organisation in Beckenham catering for people with an interest in historical subjects, and she expressed her ideas in a letter to the *Beckenham Journal*. As a result of that letter, about fifty people attended a public meeting which was held at the Central Library on Wednesday, 2 July 1947'.

Mr Tookey went on to relate how the upshot was the formation of the Branch, initially under the presidency of Alderman J.A. Bennett (see Rob Copeland's chapter on 'Personalities of Old Beckenham'). In 1949 a Local History Group emerged, with individual members assigned to particular objects of research. Prominent members of this group included Mr Edmund Roberts, who continues to serve on the Committee, and Dr Ronald Cox, now a member of the Croydon branch.

A Festival Exhibition of 'Beckenham Past and Future' was mounted in 1951 as a joint endeavour of the Branch and the Beckenham Planning Group, with financial assistance from the erstwhile Beckenham Corporation. In Coronation Year – 1953 – another exhibition was arranged, this time in collaboration with the National Women Citizens' Association, on the theme of 'The Two Elizabeths'.

Smaller exhibitions mounted by the branch (largely through the initiative of our present chairman, Dr Derek Schove) continued to be a feature in the Beckenham Library for many years around the start of each new season in September. These days, however, the main emphasis of Branch activities lies in providing a balanced programme of distinguished speakers from all parts of the country, together with a range of interesting outings, both local and longer-distance. Indeed, the variety of the activities and the support which they receive from a flourishing membership is the envy of other branches.

In the early years of the Beckenham branch (re-christened Beckenham & Bromley in 1965 to reflect municipal Beckenham's incorporation within the new London Borough of Bromley) members were appraised of forthcoming activities by attractively illustrated postcards. As numbers expanded this became impracticable, but in 1967 a monthly news bulletin was inaugurated. Despite subsequent heavy increases in the cost of postage, the *Beckenham Historian* has continued to appear without interruption.

It is unquestionably the support of the membership which has made the Beckenham & Bromley branch what it is today and, if I may conclude with the words of Geoffrey Tookey looking back in 1972 on the previous twenty-five years, 'The Branch has every reason to be pleased with the way it has secured a firm place among the societies flourishing in Beckenham and Bromley.'

ST. GEORGE'S CHURCH, BECKENHAM, KENT

Entries copied from the tombstones in the churchyard, 1976. Many Penge people were buried here as for some time this was the nearest burial ground.

1. George Bartlett, died aged 16 mths Willie Bartlett, died aged 2 yrs Sarah Jane, died Aug., 8, 1887, aged 15 yrs
2. – illegible
3. – illegible
4. Annie McWilliam, born Feb, 9th 1841, died Sept, Ist 1900
5. James Keeler, died 4th July 1875 Ann Keeler, wife of above died 22nd June 1922 Fanny Charlotte Keeler, died 30th Aug 1935 aged 70
6. John Webb, died 4th May 1875, aged 58 Thomas Webb, son killed on L.& N.W. Railway near Blisworth, Feb 21st 1864 Susannah Webb, died April 1895, aged 85
7. –
8. Christian Duncan, died 20th March, 1875, aged 1 yr 4 mths also of June Duncan, died 17th April, 1907 wife of William Duncan, died 5th April, 1914 also of Grace Duncan, died 27th Feb, 1927
9. – illegible
10. – illegible
11. James Robert Hillier, died – Harry Lowe Hillier, died –
12. John Llewellyn Evans, born 26th Sept, 1806 died 8th Jan, 1875
13. Benjamin Thomas Wild, died 8th Sept, 1874 aged 56, husband of Hannah Wild, died 7th Jan, 1892 Joseph Wild, died 10th Feb, 1886 (son) aged 41 Sarah Wild, died 9th Aug, 1886 (daughter) aged 35
14. John Hopkins, died 18th Mar, 1858 aged 67 also Maria Hopkins, died 17th Nov, 1887 wife of above.
15. – Illegible
16. Elizabeth Annie Terry, died 22nd Jan, 1874 aged 2 yrs 4 mths John Terry, died 6th Sept., 1926 aged 80 yrs Annie Terry, died 25th June, 1932 aged 88 yrs Emily Elizabeth Ashby, daughter of above died 19th, April 1955 aged 81 also Leonard Ashby, died 24th Oct, 1960 aged 86
17. Jane Maimburg, died 187– Robert Tucker, nephew died 8th Feb, 1870 aged 65 Sarah Ann Tucker, wife of above died 15th Feb, 1903 aged 89
17a. Maud Marion Lavell, died 27th Aug, 1878 aged 11 weeks 5 days Clara Eugeie Lavell, died 27th May 1885 aged 9 mths May Ethel Lavell, died 21st Sept aged 1 mth
18. Susan Pickett
19. Emma Elizabeth widow of Colonel I Dickson & daughter of Thomas Moss Tate of Toxteth Park, Liverpool died 14th May, 1873 aged 62
20. Matilda wife of William Cox, died 15th July, 1877 aged 42
21. Tom Copeland born 1869, died 1939 also Fanny Copeland born 1866, died 1941 Eliza wife of Henry Copeland, died 10th Apr 1916 aged 73 also Henry Copeland, died 20th Oct 1921
22. Margaret wife of Thomas Jones, died 25th Dec, 1872 aged 71
23. Family grave of Samuel & Mary Richards
24. Herbert Lewis, son of Daniel & Mary Richards, born 5th May, 1871 died 10th Oct 1872 Samuel Richards, died 25th Dec, 1801 also Margaret Martha Richards, daughter of above died 18th Oct, 1880 born 18th May, 1867.
25. –
26. Alfred Penny M.I.C.E. born at Bruton, Somerset 11th Oct, 1811 died Norwood 4th Mar, 1890 also Sarah wife of above of Stanmer Lodge, Beckenham, elder daughter of W.A. Weightman of Spilthorne Grove, Sunbury died 8th June, 1872 aged 57 also eldest son Alfred Penny, M. Inst. CE. born London 7th Mar, 1841 died London 7th July, 1891
27. –
28. Mary died 19th Dec, 1877 aged 18 mths also Amy Isabel, died 30th Nov, 1878 aged 5 weeks, children of E.W. & M.A. Owles and of Lucy Margaret, died 25th Feb, 1881 aged 9 mths and of Eustace Gerald Owles, son died 28th Feb, 1883 aged 10 mths.
29. M.O. 1877 A.I.O. 1878 L.M.O. 1880 E.G.O. 1883
30. Elizabeth Seymour, second daughter of John & Charlotte died 4th April, 1872 aged 7 yrs.
31. Elizabeth wife of – also Jane – died 13th Feb, 1877 also Thomas Cook.
32. – also Fanny Bird died Aug, 1876.
33. Harriett – – Walton, died Jan 1907 aged 83 also William Walton, of The Towers, Sydenham died 23rd May, 1882 aged 71.

34. Edward Clarke, died 23rd Apr, 1871 aged 43 also Mary Ann, died 27th Feb, 1915 aged 84 also James Edward, son of above died 16th Nov, 1948 aged 83.

35. William Lawrence Noakes, died Sydenham 15th Apr, 1871 aged 74.

36. William Ley Hunt, Paymaster 2nd Royal Cheshire died 10th Apr, 1871 aged 80.

37. Agnes Mylne Knilach, eldest child of -- and Harriett died Norwood April 1871 aged 12 yrs.

38. Frederick Chater, died 3rd Dec, 1870 aged 36, also Herbert Cunningham second son died Rugby, Tennessee 15th Aug, 1881 aged 19, also Francis Gerrard, died 20th Dec, 1892 aged 28, also Lucy, wife of above, also Frederick Chater – died 20th – 1918 aged –

39. –

40. Kate Sophia daughter of George & Elizabeth Boots, July 1878 also William son of above died October 18, aged 24 also Elizabeth wife of George born May 7 18?, died July 28 1884? also John Archibald Boots.

41. Clara daughter of William & Fanny Copeland died September 8 1870 aged 9 weeks, also Agnes born May 20 1873 died April 7 1875 also William died December 1911 aged 71, also Fanny died March 16 1921 aged 81.

42.

43. Hester wife of Edward Crossley died January 24 1881 aged 29 also Edward Crossley son of above died September 14 1887 aged 12.

44. Edith Beatrice Hilton died 1887.

45. –

46. Sarah wife of Alexander Mann aged 53 died January 1870 also Helen died 21 February 1873 also Alexander 1 March 1875 also Charlotte died April 18 1910.

47. Florence Kate Ambridge died wife of William Ambridge, also Mary Ann sister of above died 22nd June 1876 also William Ambridge father of above born 3rd March 1824 died 1st Nov. 1895 also Jane Ambridge wife of above died 21st Dec. 1906, age 79.

48. William Johnson died 8th April 1870, aged 47.

49. Walter Cuthbert Sweeting infant son of Thomas and Elizabeth died 24th Jan. 1870 aged 5 mths also Thomas Harry died 9th Mar. 1871 age 1 mth.

50. Ann wife of Late Walter Brind died 3rd Aug. 1863 are 72 also Walter infant son of Frederick Walter and Julia Mary Brind died 17th July 1863.

51. Mary R. L. Knight born 31st Mar. 1867 died 14th June 1922 also Herbert Theodore Knight, Canon of Rochester and Rural Dean of Bromley.

52. Hannah wife of William Bolas died 16th Oct. 1869 age 68 also William Bolas died 20th Mar. 1870 age 72.

53. Jane wife of T.A. Goodman died 6th Oct. 1869 age 70.

54. Agnes Eliza Hooker died 27th May 1868 age 11 mths also Ellen Paulina died 31st Dec. 1869 age 1 yr also John Hooker father died 29th Sept. 1878 age 43 also Mary Ann Hooker wife of above died 19th Apr. 1900 agr 68.

55. –

56. William Farr Wilson died 18th Apr. 1915 age 70 also Mary Jane died 14th May 1936.

57. Isabella daughter of James and Mary Curtis died 3rd June 1869 age 28 also James died 19th Mar. 1883 age 85 also Mary died 1890.

58. Dear little Willie died 18th Feb. 1880 age 11 mths 28 day's.

59. Georgina Margaret Barns died 17th May 1869 age 38 also Thomas Illott Barns husband died 2nd Oct. 1897 age 76.

60. –
61. –

62. George Agambar 1847–1885 also his widow Sarah Jane 1844–1932 also their daughters Rosa Mary 1872–1880 and Elizabeth Jane 1870–1886.

63. – illegible
64. – illegible
65. – illegible
66. – illegible
67. – illegible

68. Jane Christina daughter of Alexander Forbes Irvine widow of Major C.A.F. Houchen born 12th February 1825, born 20th March 1880.

69. John Simpson born 31st July 1798 died 15th May 1868.

70. William Denns died 24th February 1901 age 41 also Ellen widow of above died 22nd July 1936 age 77. also Dorothy Denns age 58 daughter of above.

71. Catherine widow of James Dennis died 19th December 1885 age 58 also of above James Dennis died 11th October 1894 age 74 also Mary Ann died 2nd February 1908 age 59 also James David husband of Mary Ann Dennis and eldest son of above James and Catherine Dennis. died 15th June 1909 age 59.

72. Elencanor Terry —˙also Mary Elliott died 8th December 1907.
73. —
74. Mary Cent widow of William Cent died 27th June 1868 age 61 also William died 31st May 1874 age 74.
75. Mary daughter of William and Sarah — also Sarah and Francis —
76. William Francis of Elmer Farm died 23rd September 1878 age 63 also Sarah died 27th January 1892 age 76.
77.
78. Sarah Budd — Joseph Budd of Lewisham died 22nd July age 50.
79. Mary Bailey died 12th June 1812 age 71 widow of John Bailey late of the parish of Chippenham Surrey.
80. Mary Ann widow of William Chichester also William Chichester born 1st May 1813 died 2nd July 1894.
81. Jane widow of John William Goldsmith died 3rd May 1868 age 28 also John William died 21st July 1863 age 38.
82. — — Catherine Weaver died 28th June 1839 age 84.
83. William Gibbons died 3rd July 1815 age 39 also Sarah died 27th October 1845 age 13.

84. Martha widow of James George Wheller died 1st May 1810 age 29 also James John son of above died August 1837 age 19 also William Edwin died 1st December 1859 also William Courteney died 1881.
85. Susanna Flint died 4th February 1821 age 13 yrs.
86. — Hockley
87. Hungerford Copelston died 7th June 1791 age 76 also Sarah Haye widow of the same place died 9th April 1805 age 75 also John Terril Hungerford Pain grandson of Sarah Haye died 19th February 1825 also Sarah Ann widow of Richard Cookes granddaughter of Sarah Haye died October 1864 also Dudley Cookes died 15th — 1879.
88. Mary Fitzherbert died 17—9 also William Fitzherbert died November 1760 age 82 also Thomas Fitzherbert died March 1762.
89. Edwin Pitt died 3rd July 1888 age 23 also Thomas Pitt died 16th July 1879 age 20 also Frederick Pitt died 3rd August 1880 age 19 Hannah Pitt widow of Edward died March 27th 1899 age 73 also Edward Pitt husband of above died 10th June 1904 age 79.
90. Thomas James died September 1860.
91. William of John and Fanny Pearce.
92. J—H 1837 W—H 1879 E—H 1889
93. L—S
94. Emily beloved daughter of Richard and Caroline Jane Duke died 9th April 1831 age 11 yrs also Richard Fenton beloved son of above died of fever on his passage home from the West Indies died 27th December 1852 age 23 also John Henry Duke brother of above died 17th February 1861 age 38 yrs.
95. James Hooker died 6th July 1837 age 28 also Eliza widow of above died 26th January 1889 aged 84 also William Harris brother in law died 14th September 1879 age 77.
96. John Keyes of Firth St. Soho died 6th November 1859 age 58 also William Addison Keyes son of above died 11th April age 19 also Selina Keyes widow of above died 21st February 1871 age 58 also Louisa Aubert daughter of above died 26th August 1880 age 39.
97. —
98. Edward Rogers born 2nd November 1834 died 3rd April 1843 also of Bessie Rogers mother of above born 7th November 1802 died 18th March 1851 also John Rogers died — 1st February 1855 age 25 also Alfred Rogers son of above died 14th July 1861 age 28 also John Rogers husband of above Bessie Rogers —.
99. Elizabeth Sarah daughter of William and Ann Rogers died 14th November 1840 age 13 also William Rogers died 19th March 181— age 72 also Ann Rogers died 9th January 1854 also William Rogers son of the above William and Ann Rogers died 15th February 1866 age 66 also Mary wife of above died— age 76.
100. Esther Rogers died 11th December 1805 age 11 mths, Ann Rogers died 4th January 1813 age 12 yrs daughter of William and Ann Rogers of this parish also Edward Rogers died 14th November 1822 age 7.
101. Mrs Elizabeth Matthew died 4th February 1847 age 72 also Michael— Michael William— and son John Matthew died 21st March 1863 age 73.
102. —

103. M.H. – .H. – . H.
104. -
105. Mrs – Matthew of Penge
106. Mary Ann Matthew died –
107. Mrs Sarah Johnson wife of Mr Joseph Johnson of St. George's in the East died 30th November 1849 age 72 also William Rogers of Selhurst Farm, Croydon died 23rd February 1877 age 49 also Sarah Rogers wife of above died 15th August 1889 age 71.
108. -
109. -
110. -
111. Eliza Sarah younger daughter of Reginald/Louisa Agnes Fowden died 5th January 1850 age 14 also above named Reginald Fowden died 26th July 1867 age 66 also Louisa Agnes wife died 18th May 1869 age 65 also Helen Amelia Murray wife of William James Kerl of Vexour, Penshurst and second daughter of above born 18th August, 1830 died 8th August 1822
112. -
113. Frederick Harris son of John/Lydia Harris, bricklayer of this parish died 9th June 1828 age 35.
114.
115. Henry Marshall died July 1922 age 79 also Mary Ann his wife died September 1929 age 86 also Ellen Louisa age 4 yrs also Henry Thomas their son age 57.
116. Eliza Jane wife of William Stone died 26th January 1855 age 52 also William Stone died 13th February 1877 age 74.
117. – .H. 1865 S.H. 1861 T.H. 1877 A.H. 1881
118. – – wife of Alexander Buff-ter died – age 36.
119. -
120. Sarah Baget died October 1827.
121. John Saxby died May 1731 age 41.
122. Elizabeth Courtney wife of Henry Reginald, Bishop of Exeter eldest daughter of Thomas 2nd Earl of Effingham died 31st October 1815 age 65 also Anne daughter died 7th December 1818 also – –.
123. Mark Noble born 22nd October 1778 died 13th November 1856 also Sophia Ri – wife born 22nd April 1785 died 15th February 1871 also Elizabeth Noble nee Lockhart wife of Mark Noble/Sophia Noble born 5th April 1811 died 19th March 1875 also her husband Mark Noble died 16th March 1881 age 69.
124. -
125. -
126. -
127. William Cassell died 5th March 1792 age 61 also Mary Cassell wife of above and younger daughter of Mark Matthew died 23rd December 1802 age 62 also Charles Jackson grandson of above died 6th December 1802 age 62 also Charles Jackson grandson of above died 6th December 1802 age 13 mths also Mark Matthew Cassell son of above died Manchester 23rd November 1830 age 54 also William son of above William/Mary Cassell died 8th November 1846 age 83 also Mrs Charlotte Rumens died 3rd November 1872 age 72 also William George Booth born 24th April 1862 died 26th October 1866.
128. -
129. Thomas Holifield died 24th November 1865 age 64 also Sarah his wife died 30th December 1861 age 62 also Thomas Holifield died 17th April 1877 age 48 also Ann Holifield died 20th June 1884 age 59.
130. Rosetta Lawrence died 30th March 1863 also Sarah Lawrence.
131.
132. Cornelius Curtis died 2nd April 1916 age 75 also Earnest George Curtis died 23rd September 1874 age 3 yrs also devoted grandmother Ellen Curtis 1847–1937.
133. James Cronk died 5th October 1831 age 53 also Hannah Cronk died 17th October 1838 age 72 also John Dennis died 9th July 1837 age 71 also his wife Hannah Barke Dennis died 2nd January 1860 age 60.
134. J.D. 1831.
135. A.S. 1812. H.S. 1817. – .S. 1850. – .S. 1857. E.S. 1863.
136. G.R. 1853.
137. Caroline Warner.
138. George Reeve died 2nd March 1853.
139. Ann Simmons wife of Humphrey Simmons died 19th July 1812 age 61 Humphrey Simmons died 6th April 1817 age 75 also Catherine Simmons daughter of above died 21st July 1860 age 72 also Elizabeth Simmons.

140. –
141. Mary Henning died 17th April 1854.
142. –
143. –
144. –
145. Samuel Homer – – also Letitia – died – January 1849 age   60.
146. –
147. – – – – died 1780. also Thomas Hatford died 1789 age 82.
148. –
149. Wake Bell son of John and Sarah – – –
150. –
151. –
152. – – Ann Grosteno died 18th Oct 1772 age 56 yrs.
153. Mary wife of John Titcombe died 14th Sept 1845 also John Titcombe died 1st May 1857 age 96 yrs.
154. William Norris bricklayer of London died 18th Nov 1751 age 26 and left behind him a disconsolate young widow after being married 5 months also of John Marriott died 29th Nov. 17 .
155. Mary wife of George Overy died 28th Aug 1811 also George Overy died 29th – ago 70 yrs also George son of above died Dec 1841 also George son of above died 18th Nov 1862 age 53 also James son of above died 12th July 1866 age 49 also Selina Mary Overy daughter of above born March died 27th March 1876 also Dinah Overy youngest daughter of above died 20th Aug 1898.
156. Mrs Jane Whitmill died 31st June 1742/3 ago 73 yrs, on her left side adjoining lieth her daughter Mrs Grace Whitmill died 30th Jan 1752 age 48.
157. –
158. – – – of Charles Sharp died March – also Charles Sharp died March.
159. William Wicker died 1714 age 58.
160. Joseph Ayres died 22nd Oct 1814 age 18 also Mrs Jane Ayres died 22nd March 1838 age 86 also Sarah Ayres daughter of above died 6th Dec 1868 age 86.
161. George Smith died 29th Mar 1828 age 19 also Elizabeth Smith mother of above died 2nd May 1855 age 75 also John Turner died 3rd April 1867 age 52 son in law of above also Elizabeth Mary Turner daughter of above.
162. –
163. –
164. A.N. 18th Feb 1867.
165. L.E.A. Wilson.
166. –
167. Humphry George – died 17th – also Ann – also William youngest son of above who died on his passage from Catalina died 13th Feb 1820 age 21.
168. Emma daughter of Edward & Jessey Williams died 28th May 1862 age 24 also Sarah Elizabeth their daughter in infancy also Jessey beloved wife of Edward Williams died 16th April 1876 age 68 also Edward Williams died 16th December 1883 age 79.
169. Charles Ryder Cooper died 29th August 18 – age 78 also William Cooper.
170. Jane Neels died 1st July 1852 age 63.
171. Mr James Eldridge of Park Street, Grosvenor Sq died 4th November 1852 age 36 also Annie Eldridge only child of above died 26th September 1852 age 1 year 8 months.
172. Mrs Amy Parrott died 10th January 1830 age 30 years also Hannah daughter of William Henry Parrott died 31st July 1841 age 1 year 8 months also Adelaide beloved daughter of Thomas Downer of Penge died 16th March 1874 age 93.
173. William White died 25th June 1888 age 47 years also Ann beloved wife of George White mother of above died 15th May 1889 age 75 also George White died 13th September 1893.
174. –
175. Harriet Mary daughter of Benjamin & Mary – of the parish of Cowley died 4th March 18 – age 8 mths also the above Benjamin died 8th Nov. –.
176. Henry Peacock died 12th July 1855 also Robert son of above died 7th November 1856 age 4 yrs also Emma second daughter of above died 30th May 1857 also Ellen 1st daughter or above died 24th July 1860.
177. – – – John Hockley.

178. –
179. – – – also William Chapman died March 1771.
180.
181. Richard East died 18– also Esther East died August 18– age 65.
182.
183. Matilda Watson Turner daughter of James & Sarah Turner died 25th May 1843 also Antoinette beloved wife of Godby Blake of Croydons' Solicitor, and sister of above died 15th March 1854 age – .
184. –
185. Richard Levens died – also Mary Levens wife of above.
186. –
187. Robert Borrowman Churchwarden 1901-1910 and of those his servants who rest in peace.
188. William Merrick surgeon many years resident of this parish, member of the Society of Friends died ––.
189. E.H. 1826. W.H. 1847.
190. Hannah wife of William Harris died 18th November – age 26 yrs also Elizabeth daughter of above died 22nd December 1826 age 18 yrs also William Harris died November 1847 age 79.
191. Kate Fanny daughter of William & – Fanny died December 1861 also Francis Alfred died 20th Oct 1869 also Louis born Feb 1876 died age 1 hour also Constance Ada –.
192. Jasper Valentine eldest son of Francis & Alice Valentine died 7th Aug. 1746 age 36.
193. Atkinson Bush died – – aged 76 also Sarah Bush wife of same also James & Edith Bush father & mother of Atkinson Bush also James Octavious Bush son of Michael & Mary Bush died 22nd Sept. 1881 aged 11 mths & 10 days also Michael Bush died 11th May 1820 age 42 also Mary daughter of Michael & Mary Eliza Bush died 1st Nov 1838 aged –7 also Mary Eliza Bush died 25th January 18–8 age 80 also Lucretia Bush died 29th Aug. 1892, aged 92 yrs also Isabella Bush died 29th April 1899 aged 87 yrs.
194. –
195. William Wilson died 15th Nov. 1827 age 65 yrs also Jannet Wilson wife of above died at Malta 17th Mar. 1836 age 92 yrs also Arther Wilson son, died 22nd Sept. 1839 aged 3 mths also William George Wilson died at Calcutta 24th June 1852 aged 29 yrs also Mary Ann Wilson died 8th Oct. 1854 aged 23 yrs also Henry Wilson died 10th Nov. – aged 30 yrs.
196. –
197. –
198. –
199. – ? – ? also Mr James Bush died 18th Mar. 1762 aged 69 yrs also Mrs Sarah Bush late of Gt. Ormond St. London.
200. Henry Batts? also William Batts? also Joseph Batts?
201. –
202. –
203. –
204. –
205. –
206. –
207. –
208. –
209. –
210. –
211. –
212. Sussanah? of James Neighbour died 24th Sept. 1871 aged 53.
213. Sarah Ann wife of Obee wife & mother died 30th Aug. 1864 aged 36 also 2 sons of above Thomas died 20th Feb. 1858 aged 14 mths also Samuel James died 22nd Jan. 1859 aged 6 yrs also Emma daughter born 8th July 1863 died 22nd Feb. 1864 also Samuel Obee husband of above born 12th Mar. 1825 died 23rd July 191 .
214. Patience Sarah eldest daughter of Edward Heavers & Christine Filby died 15th Aug. 1862 also Patience Elmer grandmother of above died 9th Mar. 1846 aged 76 also Edward Heavers Filby died 9th June 1866 aged 53 yrs.
215. Benjamin Howton of Fenchurch St. London, Tin Merchant died 20th Aug. 1759 aged 28 also on the North side of this stone lieth the body of Mr Joseph Hunt of Leadenhall St. London, died 5th Mar. 1759 aged 54 yrs.
216. –
217. –

218. William Stedman died 22nd Dec. 1846 aged 62 also Annie Rose daughter of William & Ann Sophia Dr Bruin died Good Friday 1869 aged 10 yrs also Sophia Stedman wife of above died 2nd Dec 1879 aged 92 yrs.
219. Mary Randall daughter of Stephen died 18th Oct 1694 aged 18 yrs.
220. —
221. —
222.
223. Richard May died 6th April 1862 also Charles May son of above & of Jesse Hope May died Dec. 1871.
224. Eliza daughter of William & Eliza Ovenden died 26th 1837 aged 9 mths also Sarah Harriott Teeson daughter of above — — William & Eliza Ovenden died 18th July 1866 also Eliza wife of William Ovenden died Dec. 187—. aged 66 yrs.
225. Mrs Harriot Rushton died 17th Mar. 1848 aged 42 yrs also Mr Thomas Rushton died 20th Aug. 1849 aged 43 yrs also Reginald Terry died 29th Dec. 1886 aged 64 also near this spot William Terry aged 10 yrs & George Terry aged 17 yrs sons of above Reginald Terry.
226. —
227. Joan H — — — — also Mrs Elizabeth Steward died 30th Mar. 1778 aged 77 yrs
228. Matthew White 11th Mar. age 74 yrs
229. T.B. 1852. S.B. 1834.
230. Sarah wife of Matthew White of London Sept. 1828 age — —.
231. M.A.B. 1876.
232. A.V. 1789.m
233. Robert Pratt   Emma Pratt. Edward Pratt.
234. S.W. Offer
235. M.A.P. 1878.
236. C.B. 1809., T.B. 1814., R.T. 1804.
237. M.W.T. 1843., A.B. 1854., S.T. 1855., J.T. 1855.
238. Pratt 1878.
239. Sarah of William Charlton died 1880 age 76.
240. H.G. 1836., E.G.G. 1846., S.A.G. M.C., S.F. 1880
241. William Cumberland born 18th Nov., 1795 died 28th Feb., 1881. Ann wife of above William Cumberland died 2nd Oct. — — —.
242. Lydia H — — — — died the — — — — — 180 —.
243. A.W. 18 .
244. W.C. 1843., T.U.C. 1826., J.C. 1833., C.C. 1848., E.C. 1873.
245. —. A. 1878. S.A. 1913.
246. James Vidler age 29 wife Elizabeth Vidler 29th Oct., 1810
247. Emma daughter of Thomas & Barbarer Widzell died 29th Sept. 1833 age 29 yrs Barbarer Widzell
248. Foster 1878.
249. Charles Haggart Warker born — — — — — also his wife b— — — d — — —.
250. —. —. 1808. E.T. 1832.
252. L.H. 1875. W.T. 1883. P.H. 1909.
253. J.J.V.H. 1821., C.A.T. 1832.
254. Sewell 1879.
255. S.A. 1835.
256. Jane — — — Samuel Sewell
257. A.S. 1789.
258. Ada Mary — died 20th May —   .
259. J.W. 1819., J.W., E.W. 1813., E.W. 1814.,
260. E.B. 1807
261. M.D.
262. Ann wife of George Killick died 18th Nov 1829. age 60
263. George James — husband of Frances Hall — 49 yrs Frances Hall wife — died 9th Jan 1939.
264. Constance Frances Marshall died 26th Jan 1960 — — died 21st Mar 1888 age 11 yrs Mary Ann Marshall mother died 27th Jan 1903 age 58., A.E. & M.A: Marshall.
265. Dame Louise wife of Sir John Kirkland of Queens Wood in this country & of A och, Losshire died at Beck Place 11th May 1870 born 29th Jan 1803, also their daughter Sybilla Augusta died on return from Italy — born 17th July 1821, died 6th Apr 1869, also Sir John Kirkland born 4th July 1796, died 13th Jan 1871.

266. Marie Harriette Vesie wife of Herbert A. Reed of Sydenham Road died 4th Dec 1870 also Herbert Adolphous Reed died 28th Mar 1896 age 77.

267. John Henry son of John and Ann George died 19th Apr 1878 age 3mths, also John George died 11th Mar 1909 age 73 also William George died 7th Nov 1940 age 52?.

268. – – died 15th June 1879 age 25 Mary Ann Clarke/9th Aug 1812 died Dec 1879. –

269. James Thomas Edgecombe died Nov.- 8/6" 18 age 57 also Emily Edgecombe wife of above died 10th Aug 1916 in her 78th yr also Leonard Charles Barnard grandson of above died 23rd Dec 1902 born 8th Nov 1900 also Bertie George Edgecombe second son died 17th Oct 1928 in his 57th yr also his wife Elizabeth Edgecombe died 23rd Oct 1956 age 80.

270. Joseph Oakey died Clapham 22nd May 1884 age 51 also his wife Jessie Adelaide Oakey died Jan 188 –, Helen wife of Joseph Oakey died Shorditch 8th Apr 1871 age 28.

271. Henry Crouch of Hyde, Beckenham died 29th Oct 1879 age 44 also Ida Muriel Crouch of Hyde, Esher died 18th June 1955 age 84 also Ida Muriel Crouch died 13th May 1961 age 84.

272. Admiral Horatio Beauman Young born 24th Apr 1806 died 17th Dec 1879.

273. Rebecca Thorogood died Sept –

274. Percy George – William – Goodman

275. Jeremiah Green died 13th Mar 1897 age 67 James Green son of above died 30th Mar 1873 age 14 mths Sarah Green wife of above died 6th Dec 1934 age 97.

276. Henry Augustus Hoadley son of John and Mary Ann Hoadley of Penge Park, died 10th Aug 1878 age 32, also Emily Sophia widow- died 8th Sept 1941 age 87, also Helena Augustus, daughter of above died 2nd Jan. 1953 age 74.

277. George John Hibbins born 7th Oct 1869 died 24th Feb 1873 also Rebecca Hibbins born 12th Aug 1873, died 22nd Jann 1874, George Hibbins father, born 18th Jan., 1837 died 1st Mar., 1880, also Eleanor wife of – died 2nd Sept. 1902 age 6 –, also Henry Milland Hibbins – – –.

278. Edwin William Goodman died Aug 25th 1877 age 60.

279. Elizabeth Stewart

280. George Gower age 41 Alexander E. Killick died Sept. 1912 age 76.

281. Eldred Harry Littlehales died 12th Jan 1897 also Emma his wife died 12th Oct. 1924 age 97.

282. Marther wife of George Sameson died 5th Dec 1882 age 56, also Albert, 2nd son of above died 19th Mar. 1879 age 20, also George Sampson died 11th Oct. 1887 age 76.

283. Robert John Davis died 25th Oct. 1901 age 53 yrs, also is daughter Emma L. Davis – also Sarah Tyson Davis died 1st Sept. 1914 age 70.

284. Charles Wright died July 1877.

285. James Coe of Kent House Tavern, Beckenham died Jan. 1878, age 36, also Minnie Sarah Hellen Coe infant daughter of above died 14th Mar. 1871 age 8 mths

286. Betsy Wood died 20th Sept. 1877 age 26. William Wood died 14th Sept. 1929 age 82, John Wood died 1st Aug 1930 age 84,

287. Edwin Godwin

288. John Hudson and Ann his wife died 2nd and 3rd Feb. 1907 both aged 83.

289. Frederick Ambridge 1863–1946– 60 yrs chorister Harold Ambridge 1893–1896 also Hilda 1899–1936 Ada E. Ambridge born 30th July 1868 died 4th Feb. 1955.

290. John Pilbeam died 9th Oct. 1885 age 65 also Hannah Pilbeam his wife died 23rd Dec., 1887 age 80.

291. William Jeffs died 16th Oct. 1894 age 51. Grace Jeffs died 19th June 1871 age 3 weeks Andrew Jeffs died 17th July 1884 age 2½ yrs. William eldest son died 21st May 1895 age 22. Sarah Jeffs wife of William died – – age 63.

292. Lily daughter of Thomas & Caroline Jones of Beckenham died 31st May 1877 age 10 mths, also Mabel died 12th Feb 1880 age 11 mths also Daisy May died 22nd Apr 1887 age 6 yrs also Douglas George died 23rd May 1888 age 4 yrs.

293. Alfred Harrison, Priest, born 8th May 1832 died 19th Dec. 1891 also his wife Edith Grace Harrison died 7th Apr. 1937 age 91.

294. John Philip Laurence, born 1st, Nov 1829, died 7th Oct 1890, also Evelyn Laurence wife of above, 4th May 1844, died 20th Oct. 1926, also Percival John Laurence died 19th Jan. 1888 age 21, also Mary Evelyn Laurence died 21st Feb 1955 age 87.

295. Amos Parks Jane Parks died 1880 Merry Amy Jane Parks Ethel Jane Parks died 188 – George Amos Parks

296. George Augustus Parkyns born 29th Nov. 1859 also Sir Thomas G.A. Parkins born 28th June 1820, died 7th Mar 1895.

297. John Dennis sextons verger for 40 yrs, died 5th Jan 1928 age 73 also Annie Jane Dawson born 1st Oct. 1864, died 11th June 1936, also Ann Dennis wife, died 4th Mar. 1913 R.I.P.

298. Henry Neve Goodhart born Langley Park 26th Oct. 18 –, died sunrise 11th Oct. 1880, also Leslie Neve Goodhart 2nd son, died 30th Dec. 1890 age 12, also Alice Marrion wife born 12th May 1852, at Bilbao, Spain, died 31st Dec 1839 at Windsor, Berkshire.

299. Amelia Hawkins born 28th Aug 1868, died 28th June 1880, also Ann Hawkins mother of above, died 17th June 1887 age 53, also James Hawkins husband of above died 7th Nov. 1926, age 86, also George Hawkins, son, died 30th July 1946, born 1868.

300. Ernest Henry, born 25th Dec 1872, died 25th Apr. 187– eldest child of Tom & Sarah Jane Armstrong – grandchild Henry Russell and Sarah Ellis also Alfred George, brother of above died 10th July 1889 age 7 mths, also Eleanor Mary Naomi Hambrook younger daughter of H.R. & S. Ellis, died 12th June 1887 age 30, also Sarah Ellis wife of H.R. Ellis of High St., died 25th May 1897 age 73, also Henry Russell Ellis died 5th Oct. 1902 age 72.

301. Doris Mary wife of Charles Davenport died 30th May 1880 also Charles Davenport died 21st Feb. 1890.

302. Mary Augusta Powys infant son of Edward and Mary Mathers, died 29th Mar. 1897 age 10 mths, also Amelia Isles Mathers died 13th May, 1926 age 80.

303. Margaret Mindenhall born 27th Oct. 1847, died 21st Dec. 1928, also Thomas Mindenhall died 5th Sept. 1934 age 82.

304. Sarah Forbes died 24th May 1880.

305. Harriett Staunton – 1877.

306. William Wright died 7th Apr. 1879 age 64 yrs.

307. Harriett Isabel wife of Lee Steere died 2nd Nov. 1877 age 36, also Ellen Steere died 19th Feb. 1879 age 44.

308. Elizabeth James died 6th Mar. 1900 age 74 also Emily James died 7th Jan. 1911 age 69 also Sarah James died 28th May 1912 age 75 also Alice Brown died 27th Feb. 1924 age 61.

309. Constance Adelaide infant daughter of Fred and Janie Cutbill, born 13th Mar. 1880, died 13th Aug. 1880;

310. Elizabeth Groombridge June 1879 age 34.

311. Norton Thatcher died – Jan. 1903 age 76 & two children, also Harriett wife died 1st July 1932 age 81.

312. Ann Susannah wife of George Bishender died 16th May 1881 age 49, also Elizabeth Amelia Bishender, died 21st Oct 1946, age 73.

313. Henry Thomas Crayford died 21st May 1880 age 48, also Harriett his wife died 7th June 1886 age 53.

314. Robert McMorland of Ridgemount, Beckenham died 23rd Dec 1879 age 57, also Elizabeth his wife, died at Croydon 17th Jan. 1898 age 65, also Elizabeth Sarah McMorland, 2nd daughter of above died Croydon, 9th Aug. 1941 age 70, also Katharine McMorland, eldest daughter died at Croydon, 22nd Feb. 1946 age 89. R.I.P.

315. Hugh Wilson died 25th Sept. 1888 age 60, also Harriett Martha, wife of above died 22nd July 1904 age 84, also Elizabeth Ann Wilson elder daughter of Hugh Wilson, also Guillermo Andres, son of Hugh Wilson, died Rio De Janeiro, 7th Mar. 1893 age 40.

316. John Cumberland died 9th Mar. 1887 age 53, also Ann Cumberland, widow, died 28th Mar. 1922 age 84.

317. John Kinaman Esq, died 18th Aug. 1878 age 49.

318. Sarah Sexton died 27th Oct. 1888 age 46.

319. William Bennett died 7th Oct. 1874 age 37, also his wife Elizabeth Bennett died 3rd Dec. 1887 age 53, also Robert Bennett died 22nd June 1870 age 3 yrs also George Bennett eldest son, died 1st Sept 1887 age 28, – – stone by J. Andrews, Beckenham.

320. Michael Moore, 15 years Churchwarden, died 18th Jan. 1892 age 74, also Jane his wife, died 18th Nov. 1900 age 87, also his son Francis Michael died 22nd Dec. 1908 at Portland, Oregan, U.S.A. also Thomas Maybank Webb, died 27th Mar. 1928 age 60, also Jane Moore, daughter of Michael Webb, died 13th Feb. 1933 age 85.

321. William Adams Stevens, born 9th Dec. 1820, died 28th Jan. 1878, also William son of W.A. Stevens, born 14th Apr 1851, died at Brighton, 19th Mar. 1926 also Anna Maria wife of W.A. Stevens, born 26th July 182–, died 10th Feb. 1907, also Edith, died daughter of W.A. Stevens died 22nd Sept. 1934.

322. Arthur DeBruin died 16th Apr. 1877 age 26, also William De Bruin died 10th Aug. 1890 age 78, also Ann Sophia DeBruin died 10th Dec. 1917 age 97, also Arthur James DeBruin – – gave his life for his country 1916.

323. Edward Harold Thompson died 20th July 1879 age 6 .

324. Thomas Evans – – – also Maria – Feb. 19, 1896 died – age 81

325. William Lucas Merry born 29th Feb. 1824, died 18th Feb. 1893, also Mary wife of above born 9th May 1833, died 5th Aug. 1901.

326. Violet Mary, born Innocents Day 1876, died 16th Sept. 1878, daughter of Henry Tindal and Amy Atkinson.
327. Sarah Anne Cother wife died 12th Dec. 1914, also Frederick Cadogan Barrow died 4th Aug. 1904, also Violet Elise Needham Barrow, died 28th Sept. 1906.
328. Ann –
329. – – – – 1904
330. Robert Edward Barnes born at Iken, Suffolk, 1st Feb. 1812, buried at Beckenham 6th Dec. 1877, also Edward Fulton son of – died New Zealand, 3rd July 1897 age 37, also Louisa Sophia –
331. Sarah –
332. Edward Holledge died at Penge, 31st Mar. 1876, age 55, also Mary Holledge wife – died 11th June 1901.
333. Mary Purvis died – Dec. 1894, Charles Purvis died 1st Dec. 1915, Mary Purvis died Jan. 1917.
334. Mary Woldrond died 1st Dec. 1927 age 86, Theodore Henry Maine Waldrond died 13th Apr. 1875 age 32.
335. Margaret Suter Atkinson died at Norwood, 17th Feb. 1875, widow of Thomas James Atkinson drowned near the Cape of Good Hope on his passage from India, May 1864.
336. Robert Borrowman died 24th Aug. 1910 age 46, Agnes Borrowman died Sept. 1949.
337. Jane of Robert Edmund Morrice died at Blackheath, 15th Jan. 1875 age 64, Caroline Payne Hubbard, sister in law died 27th June 1882 age 75, also Guy infant son of James and Therese Jane Calvert, 9th grandson of Jane Morrice died 24th June 1889 age 3 weeks, also Robert Edmund Morrice, husband of Jane Morrice, died – Mar. 1892.
338. ? D mot Harrison born 1795, died 18th Dec. 1873, Annah Harrison died 1882.
339. Catherine Eupha Skinner born 4th Aug. 1895, died July 1896, Hilton Skinner born 5th Jan. 1862, died 6th Mar. 1928, also Catherine his wife born 4th Aug. 1864, died 8th Apr. 1937, Douglas Hilton Skinner B.A. born 20th June 1896
340. George Crawshaw died 10th Sept. 1896. , also Robert Henry Crawshaw died 28th Aug. 1896.
341. Arthur Henry John Johnstone late Cptn. R.N., died 24th July 1874 age 39, Elizabeth Johnstone died 20th Jan. 1922 age 76.
342. James MacDonell born 21st Apr. 1841, died 2nd Mar. 1873.
343. Henry Brown died 22nd Jan. 1914 age 77, Frances Mary Brown wife of above died 17th Dec. 1916 age 77, George Ernest Brown youngest son, died 24th Feb. 1875 age 1 yr 5 mths, Agnes Louisa Brown younger daughter died 31st Dec. 1937 age 70, Raymond V. Brown eldest son, died 8th Nov. 1959.
344. Henry William Lovelock M.N. 1st Batt. 7 London Regt., also Annie wife of William Lovelock died 20th Feb. 1900 age 62, also William Lovelock died 17th Oct. 1897 age 57, also Sgt., H.W. Lovelock M.M. 1/7 London Rgt. Godson of William killed on the Somme, 7th Oct. 1916 age 26.
345. Bouverie Campbell born Nov. 1852, died 1st Oct. 1879, also John M.C. Campbell of R. A. died in India 22nd July 1875 age 50, also Grace Lilian, eldest child of Alex Campbell and niece of Col. Campbell died 6th Dec. 1879 age 11
346. –
347. Frederick Man died 30th Jan. 1887 age 71, Emma Harriett Man wife died 25th July 1913 age 81.
348. Effie Ella, 3rd daughter of T.H. & A. Clarke died 19th May 1923 age 55, Edith Florence Clarke elder daughter of Theophilus Hughes Clarke & Anabella Clarke died 29th Oct. 1936 also Theophilus Hughes Clarke died 18th Apr. 1897 age 68, Anabella Clarke died 2nd Dec. 1916 age 71.
349. John Manger born Canterbury, died 1st Jan. age 79, also wife Elizabeth, died 18th Aug. 1897 age 95, also Ellen Elizabeth Manger, died age 84, 3rd Nov. 1915, also Emily Ann Manger died 1st Jan. 1926 age 96, also Esther Ann died 26th Mar. 1940 age 90.
350. John Edward Mahood
351. –
352. Hon. Emily Eden daughter of William 1st Lord of Auckland died 5th Aug. 1869 age 72.
353. Thomas and Emiley – – – Mary Anset
354. –
355. William Atkinson of son of Joseph Atkinson of Manchester, 17th July 1825 8th Apr. 1907-40 yrs resident of Beckenham, and Anne Sophia Atkinson daughter of Samuel Jowett Birchall of Leeds, 1st Sept. 1830– 8th Apr. 1905, wife of William Atkinson, Hilda Sophia, 15th Sept. 1871- 18th Dec. 1871, child of William and Anna Sophia

356. Letitia Landsdown died 5th Aug. 1889 age 82, also Emma Letitia Nicholls died 20th Mar. 1875 age 4, George Ernest McHolls died 11th July 1878 age 7 mths child of William & Jane Nicholls and godchild of above.

357. Henry Phillips Thomas of Newfoundland, born 25th Sept. 1791, died 10th Aug. 1872, also Louisa Dixon died 8th Jan. 1877 age 76, Henry Charles Binney Thomas, nephew of Henry Phillips Thomas born Newfoundland, 5th Oct. 1822, died 29th Mar. 1907.

358. Eliza Bealey Chubb wife of John Chubb, born 19th Feb. 1836, died 30th June 1903, John Chubb of St. Pauls churchyard, Brixton Rise, born 15th Nov. 1815 died 30th Oct. 1872.

359. Herbert Arnand Taylor- 12 Melbury Road, Kensington, youngest son of Watkin Williams and Amelia Taylor, born 3rd Aug. 1841, died 23rd Dec. 1915, also Amelia wife of Watkin Williams Taylor of Ashurst House, Sydenham, born 4th Apr. 1799, died — July 1877, also Watkin Williams Taylor husband, born 28th Feb. 1805, died 19th June 1878.

360. Francis Sewell died 22nd June 1889 age 54, Ada Sewell daughter, died 21st Dec. 1875 age 3 yr 6 mths, also Charlotte Sewell wife of above, died 19th Jan. 1914 age 76.

361. Tom William Thornton died 15th Feb. 1933 age 77, also wife Clara died 31st July 1935 age 76, Constance Mary, eldest daughter, died 29th Dec. 1956, also Hedley Thomas, eldest son of Tom William And Clara Thornton, 2nd Lt. 5th. Btn. Royal West Kent Regt., born 16th Sept. 1882, died 25th Jan. 1916, also Gertrude Fanny Thornton- 1886 --1961, Frank Thornton- 1885–1966, Edith M. Thornton– 1890–1971, Private Stanley Thornton killed in France, 3rd May 1917 age 19.

362. Thomas Peache died 1785 age 65, also John Peache died 5th Mar. 1771 age 68.

363. Eleanor Sophia daughter, – Matthew and Sarah age 8 – – Mathew Whi also Maria – – – Harriett Bengal Cavalry, died Brighton

364. Theresa, youngest daughter of Vice Admiral Sir Edward Griffith Colpoys K.C.B. and Wife of Alexander Beattie Esq., of the Wood, Sydenham Hill, died 30th Jan. 1854 age 43, also Harriett Elizabeth, 2nd daughter of Alexander and Theresa Beattie, died 20th May 1854 age 45, also Alexander Beattie Esq, Kingston 10th July 188- age 82.

365. Charlotte wife of William Whitmore esq., born 30th June 1795, died 15th Feb, 1855, also William Whitmore, born 24th Mar. 1795, died 17th June 1869.

366. Thomas Pearce of St. James Lodge, Beckenham, died 20th Nov. 1866 age 68, also William 4th son of above, died 9th Feb 1873 age 41, also Alfred Benjamin, 2nd son, died 26th Oct. 1890 age 66, also Elizabeth Ann, wife of Thomas Pearce, also Arthur – –

367. M. Thomas Burningham July also Sarah wife of Henry

368. Louisa wife of Thomas Clear died 11th Oct. 1863 age 31, also her brother Edmond Jefferies died 21st May 1864 age 28, also Louisa Anne Roche Clear daughter of Thomas and Louisa Clear died 20th Sept. 1872 age 19, also Thomas Clear died Lewisham 21st July 1882 age 56 yrs.

369. Maria widow of Major Edward Hodge 7th Hussars, daughter of Sir Edmund Bacon premier Baronet of Raveningham, Norfolk, died 27th Jan. 1864 age 79, also Eleanor Hodge, youngest daughter of Major Hodge, born 11th Sept. 1812, died 11th Oct. 1874, also Caroline Hodge – 2nd daughter, born 7th Aug. 1811, died 10th Oct. 1898.

370. –

371. The family of William Stephen Watton of Woodside, Croydon, Surrey, – John Watton youngest son of W.S. Watton died 2nd Oct. 1817 age 3 yrs.

372. – Watton also Maria Watton, also William Stephen Watton died 13th Feb. 1841.

373. –

374. John 1779

375. –

376. M. James Squires died 23rd Apr. 1762 age 40

377. – John Brown, Elizabeth Brown

378. –

379. Cecilia Charlotte daughter of William and Mariane Peters born 17th – 1837 died – Jan. 1840.

380. Andrew Brandram 1790 also Elizabeth his wife, also Mary Ann, also Maria wife of Andrew Babbs youngest son of Andrew Brandram born 26th Mar. 1840 died 20th June 1871.

381. –

382. Deborah wife of Thomas Poole died 21st July 1812 age 75, also Thomas Poole died 22nd Jan. 1813 age 75, also Richard Poole son of above, died 4th June 1829, also Sarah Poole wife of Richard Poole died 15th July age 74.

383. John Cator of Beckenham Place died 21st Feb. 1806 age 76, also Mary Cator his wife died 13th Aug. 1804 age 71, also Maria, only child died – April 1766 aged 3 yrs, also Mary his mother died 26th Aug. 1787 age 78, also Ann his siter died 27th July 1766 age 17, also Mary daughter of brother Samuel died Aug. 1793 age 8.

384. –

385. –

386. Cecil Frederick Joseph Jennings died 5th Feb. 1946 age 90, also his wife Jessie Jennings died 10th Mar. 1958 age 91.

387. Jessie Clara Spence wife of Horace Spence died 9th Oct. 1918 age 67, also their daughter Jessie Spence died 11th Jan. 1946, also Margaret Spence – 1884–1968, also Horace Robert Spence died at Angers 14th July 1931 age 79.

388. Evelyn Julia wife of Edward R. Allfrey died 28th Sept. 1887 age 44.

389. Violet Edith Fanny Lendon died 8th Apr. 1903. also William Henry Lendon died 23rd Sept 1915 age 65.

390. –

391. –

392. William Whitwell died 1823 age –

393. Sarah – – died June 1821, John – –, Catherine Dinsdale died Feb. 1839 age 72, Catherine daughter of above – – age 92.

394. Elizabeth Churcher died 9th Mar. 1887 age 75, also William Churcher died 7th Mar. 1890 age 73, also Emma Elizabeth Churcher daughter, born 31st Jan. 1844 died 19th Feb. 1942, also Fanny Churcher born 23rd May 1853, died 4th Mar. 1943.

395. John Hum–

396. –

397. Victor Thornton born 29th Jan. 1902– died 24th May 1963.

398. Frances wife of Charles Alsager Elgood died 4th Dec. 1934, also Charles Alsager Elgood died 22nd July 1945.

399. Julia Maling wife of J.F.T. Dipnall esq, died at Hastings, 9th Nov. 1867 age 37.

400. John Berry Torry born 3rd Mar. 1836– died – Mar. 1917, also Cardross Grant born 30th Apr. 1845–died 31st Dec. 1916, also Sophia Harriett Grant died 15th July 1940.

401. –

402. – – – born 19th Apr. 1833, died – – age 70.

403. James Athans died 1902 age 68.

404. Bertie Peter Cator born 29th Feb. 1836 died 30th Mar. 1875, also Mary his wife born – Dec. 1833, died 1st Jan. 1918.

405. Isabel Anne Cator died 27th May 187– age 34

406. Alfred Norton 2nd son of Richard and Domica Elizabeth Stevens died 29th June 1872 age 17½ mths, also Louisa Elizabeth Stevens died 29th Dec. 1911 age 75, also Richard Stevens died 13th Nov. 1939 age 94, also Laura Stevens 3rd daughter of above died 13th Feb. 1931 age 63, also Sarah Phoebe, wife of Herbert Stevens died – Nov. 1938 age 76, also Richrd Stevens died 6th Jan. 1946 age 81.

407. –

408. –

409. Edward Francis died 11th June 1935 age 76, also Mary Ellen Francis age 83

410. Abraham Bayliss, Emily Bayliss, John Bayliss, Maria Johanna Haymes

411. Charlotte Vian of Fairview, Beckenham wife of William J. Vian born 24th Jan. 1877, died 22nd June 1938, also William John Vian born 31st Mar. 1827 died 25th Mar. 1890, also William Collett Vian eldest son, died Jan. 1931, also Marian Vian died Dec. 16th, 1934, also Maud Margaret Vian, daughter born 5th July 1868, died 28th June 1881, also Charlotte Vian died 7th Dec. 1951.

412. Elizabeth wife of John Ward died 14th Mar. 1881, also John Ward age 84, survived his wife by 1 day.

413. Henry Charles Roberts, Major Bengal Infantry, died 24th Feb. 1880 age 63.

414. –

415. –

416. –

417. Elizabeth Biggs born 18th Jan. 1798, died 1st Dec. 1856 age 36

418. –

419. 1867496, Flt, Sgt. J.E. Overfield-Collins, Flt. Eng. R.A.F. 6th Nov. 1945 age 21.

420. Rebecca wife of George Cowen died 22nd July 1896 age 38

421. John Cuthbert Stenning born 5th Jan. 1839, died at Bath 12th Feb. 1922, buried at – Eastbourne, Churchwarden 1892–1901.

422. Thomas Marshall brother of John Marshall died 14th Aug. 1866 age 64, – Marshall of Beckenham died 1864 in his 69th year.
423. Alexander Harley youngest son of Alexander Harley Maxwell of Pontpack, Dumfrieshire, died Beckenham 23rd Aug. 1876 age 52, also Constance Harley daughter of Alexander and Catherine Harley died 16th Dec. 1864 age 8 mths.
424. Winifred Emily Wotherspoon died 24th Aug. 1941 age 43.
425. Henry Hamond Gregory died 19th Apr 1940, also his wife Edyth, died 6th Dec. 1941.
426. William Laver died 4th May 1935 age 79, also his wife Hanna Beatrice Laver died 5th May 1936 age 78, also William James Laver died 11th Oct. 1963 age 81.
427. Thomas Mansfield died 8th June 1811 age 71, also Rebecca Mansfield daughter of John and Thomas Banth?
428. Mary Ann Perram died 13th Jan. 1888.
429. Elizabeth Scott Hockin – – 5th May 1927, John Hockin died Sept. 1893 age 33
430. Mary Ann Perram – 13th Jan. 1888, also Lydia Perram died in Poonah, India, 25th Aug. 1891.
431. –
432. Charlotte Elizabeth wife of Lister Beck died 14th Oct. 1894, – – – died Clara Lucy, died 29th Oct. 1937 age 78.
433. Samuel Sidney Carr died 13th Aug. 1842, age 1 yr, 9 mths, also James Joshua Carr of Old Charlton, Kent, died 22nd May 1865 age 67, also Harriet Catherine widow of above also Cpt. James Sweet Carr, Bombay Staff Corps, died 28th Feb. 1864 age 31, also Harriet Catherine Romanoff daughter of James Joshua and Harriet Catherine Carr, died 10th Aug. 1897 age 69, at Kishinieff, Russia, also Jane Susan Carr daughter of James – –
434. Frederic William Petch died 8th Feb. 1937 age 70 also his wife Annie Petch died July 1937 age 74.
435. Ellen Rebecca Booth of Anerley died 8th Feb. 1896 age 52, also Harriet Booth died 20th Dec. 1874 age 2 also Frederick Booth died 21st Dec. 1895 age 4.
436. Rosalie Elizabeth Davies died 20th Nov. 1940 age 82, also Herbert Foster Davies died 18th Feb. 1928 age 74.
437. Albert Roy Sullivan died 12th Feb. 1953 age 65, chorister
438. Major General Granville Anson Chetwynd Starylton died 2nd Dec. 1831 age 76 yrs.
439. Vault of Edward Richard Adams esq 1856.
440. Abraham Adgall? – – – Mary
441. Thomas Clark – – age 7, John Clark ,
442. – – Rob Bathurst of Horsted in the county of Norfolk, died at Beckenham 27th Dec. 1841 age 44
443. Samuel Brooker of Croydon, Surrey died 14th Aug. 1826, – – wife Vel Brooker – – – also Bendry Brooker – – Henry Brooker died 1869
444. James Farish youngest son of Professor Farish of Cambridge
445. Edward Gwyn, carpenter, citizen of London, of the parish of St. Mary, Whitechapel, died 24th Nov. 1745 age 53, also lyeth John Gwyn, brother of Edward Gwyn died 25th March 17 – –
446. Jane Baxter died – – age 34, also Anna Baxter –, also Harriet Jane Pilbeam daughter of above, also James Pilbeam died Oct. 1872 age 30
447. John Wilford, citizen of London, – – John Wilford, son died 13th Aug. 1740 age 4
448. Thomas Chapman died 17th Aug. – age 55, also John Chapman died 6th Oct. 1775 age 42
449. William Arlott – – died 1872 age 45, 30 yrs gardener to Joseph Cator Esq whose family erected this stone.
450. –
451. G.P. died 15th Jan. 1832 age 18 mths
452. Charles Drummond Esq of 17, Stratton Street, London, died 23rd Aug. 1858 age 67, also The Hon. Mary Dulcibella, widow, 6th daughter of William, 1st Lord Auchland, died 20th March 1862 age 68, also Mary Dulcibella, daughter of Charles and Mary Dulcibella Drummond, widow of Richard Wellesley esq, born 18th Aug. 1827, died – Aug. 1874, also Robert Drummond died 29th April age 58
453. –
454. Gertrude Dorothy Curwen, – – Henry and Sophia Fanny Curwen born 2nd Oct. 1887, died
455. Elizabeth Philips wife of T.C. Cole, born New Orleans, 28th Oct. 1839, died 18th Dec. 1923, also Thomas Charles Cole, – – born Stratford on Avon 1859.
456. Ada Mary O'Grady died 20th June 1932, also David Patrick, husband, died 15th Jan. 1964, also Winifred Ethel, Sister of Ada Mary, wife of Arthur Ford died Oct. 1957, Melbourne, Australia.

457. Joseph Cator died 14th Jan. 1818 are 84, his widow, Diana, died 14th May 1829 age 72, also their eldest son John, died 20th Aug. 1848 age 76, also 2nd son Albermarles, died 26th Nov. 1796 age 42, also Admiral Bertie Cornelius, 5th son, died 23rd July 1864 age 76, also Thomas, 6th son, Rector of Kirksmeaton, and Vicar of Womersley, Yorkshire, died 24th April 1864, age 74, also Diana, eldest daughter, died 5th Apr. 1817 age 33, also Emily Ann, died Apr. 1815 age 3, also Sophia wife of Bertie, died 15th Nov. 1862 age 74, also Jane Bradford widow, died 24th Aug. 1796, age 46, also Mary Delafield, widow, died 11th Mar. 1808 age 51, Also Peter Cator, 7th son died 1st May 1873, age 77, his wife Martha Cator died 9th June 1872, age 73 also Diana Cator, daughter, died 3rd Oct. 1888 age 63, also Charles Oliver Frederick Cator, son of Thomas Cator, died 10th Dec. 1876 age 40, also Lady Louisa Frances, daughter of John, 7th Earl of Scarborough, wife of the Rev Thomas Cator, died 7th Jan. 1885 age 90, also Bertie Cornelius Cator, Lieut. R.N. eldest son of Bertie and Sophia Cator, died 26th Aug. 1842, whilst in service in the China Seas, age 25, buried in Golden Island near Nankin, China.

458. Major Edward Jones died June 1889 age 62, Ile/Nob Vere – – wife of Edward Vereesq 1880 age 81

459. Frederick Silver died 7th Oct. 1864 age 82, also F.S. Silver died 21st June 1866 age 53, also Hannah widow of Frederick Silver died 4th Jan. 1868 age 80

460. –

461. –

462. –

463. –

464. Gle – Randall Brown – – daughter of above – – also Elizabeth Brown late of Dulwich died 9th Apr. 1859 age –, also John Brown K.C.V., also Elizabeth Brown Nov. 1855, Elizabeth wife of Samuel Brown, – Samuel Brown – – – – Mar. 1855

465. Mary wife of George Eoskey of the 25th Regt. died 3rd Jan. 1861 age 66

466. John Dudin Brown of Sydenham died Hastings, age 59, Mar. 1855, also wife Ann – – died 29th Oct. 1855 age 56 yrs.

467. Elizabeth Chorlton formerly of Chester, but later Shortlands, died 9th May 1867 age 48.

468. Elizabeth Woodrooffe died 1840, age 69, also Martha Woodrooffe died Sept. 1842 age 83.

469. Elizabeth Gordon widow of Lieut Col. Gordon

470. Sophia Fanny Curwen died May 1909 age 57, also Robert Curwen died Mar. 1945 age 70, also Gertrude Dorothy infant daughter of Henry and Sophia Curwen born Oct. 1887, died Aug. 1888.

471. Robert Ratheram Stilwell M.D., born 26th June 1834, died 28th Dec. 1887, also Angela Emma Mary wife of above, born 8th July 1837, died 22nd Mar. 1902 also Spencer Fabris Stilwell, youngest son of – – born 4th Nov. 1875 died – May 18 – –

472. Charles Elton Coulborn born 19th Feb. 1843, died 14th Sept. 1887.

473. –

474. Louisa Maria Sophia Cator born 26th Sept. 1830, died 11th Apr. 1886

475. Ann Drussilla wife of Edwin Covell of Beckenham Place, died 18th July 1889, age 51, also Edwin Covell of B.P. – May – – age 57.

476. Sacred to the memory of Susana wife of Edward King died 17th June 1821.

477. Charles Henry – –

478. Charles Austin – – – also Elizabeth Hougden Austin Widow of above died 1st May – 20 age 34.

479. Henry Austin died 18th Feb 1883

480. Mary Austin died 14th Feb. 1908 age 63, also Flora Mary, 2nd daughter of above died 13th Sept. 1912 age 25, also Charles Thomas, husband of above Mary Austin died 21st Dec. 1917 age 77, also Elizabeth Emily, elder daughter of above died 23rd Jan. 1923 age 50, also Charles William Austin died 14th Nov. 1958 age 79.

481. –

482. –

483. Henry B –   also Elizabeth B

484. –

485. Alice Mary Cobb

486. Hannah – – William

487. **John Pearce Self died 7th Sept 1882 age 71**